## BOOKS BY ALBERT MARRIN

*The Airman's War*
*Overlord*
*Victory in the Pacific*
*The Secret Armies*
*The Sea Rovers*
*War Clouds in the West*
*1812: The War Nobody Won*
*Aztecs and Spaniards*
*The Yanks Are Coming*
*Struggle for a Continent*
*The War for Independence*

# *The* WAR *for*
# INDEPENDENCE

# The WAR *for* INDEPENDENCE

## The Story of the American Revolution

## by Albert Marrin

New York · ATHENEUM · 1988

JAN 3 1991

Picture Credits

National Archives: frontis, 13, 20, 30, 32, 41, 50–51, 52–53, 72–73, 81, 84, 98–99, 106, 114, 117, 120, 125, 131, 146–147, 152, 163, 165, 170–171, 206, 209, 239, 242, 250, 262–263, 265

*The American Revolution: A Picture Sourcebook* (Dover): 39, 100, 133, 136, 141, 194, 202, 220, 244, 253

The maps on pages 10–11, 48–49, 62–63, 94–95, 108–109, and 128–129 are from *Atlas of American History*, Revised edition edited by Kenneth T. Jackson, used with the permission of Charles Scribner's Sons. Copyright 1943, © 1978 Charles Scribner's Sons; copyright renewed © 1971 Charles Scribner's Sons.

*Atheneum*
*Macmillan Publishing Company, 866 Third Avenue, New York, NY 10022*
*Collier Macmillan Canada, Inc.*

*Text set by Arcata Graphics/Kingsport, Kingsport, Tennessee*
*Printed and bound by Fairfield Graphics/Fairfield, Fairfield, Pennsylvania*
*Designed by Mary Ahern*
*First Edition*

10   9   8   7   6   5   4   3   2

*Library of Congress Cataloging-in-Publication Data*

Marrin, Albert.
The war for independence.

Includes index.
Bibliography: p. 267.
A detailed account of the Revolutionary War beginning
with its origins in the French and Indian War.
1. United States—History—Revolution, 1775–1783—
Juvenile literature. [1. United States—History—Revolu-
tion, 1775–1783]   I. Title.
E208.M348   1988       973.3       87-13711
ISBN 0-689-31390-X

*This book is dedicated, with appreciation,
to the National Cristina Foundation
and their revolutionary ideas
about independence.*

# Contents

It is impossible to *beat* the notion of liberty
out of these people. It is rooted in 'em from
childhood.

—*General Thomas Gage*

It will not be believed that such a force as
Great Britain has employed . . . could be baffled
. . . by numbers infinitely less, composed of men
oftentime half-starved, always in rags, without
pay, and experiencing every species of distress
which human nature is capable of undergoing.

—*George Washington*

# *The* WAR *for*
# INDEPENDENCE

# The Virginian

*M*ORNING, May 4, 1775.
A dazzling spring morning in Virginia. Gentle, warm breezes bring the scent of wildflowers and freshly cut grass. The Potomac River flows lazily, pinpoints of sunlight dancing among the swirls and ripples.

A grand plantation house with white pillars overlooks the river from a high bluff, Mount Vernon. In the driveway is a carriage loaded with the master's luggage, its wooden panels and brasswork polished to a high gloss. The four-horse team waits patiently in harness, occasionally flicking tails to worry the blue and green horseflies.

As a black houseboy held open the carriage door, George Washington turned to his wife, Martha. He was her "Old Man," she his darling "Patsy." They were the same age, forty-three, and although married sixteen years, they had no children; Martha did have two children, a boy and a girl, from an earlier marriage. They loved each other very much, and he always wore a miniature painting of her under his shirt, next to his heart.

They'd often said good-bye, for he was an important

man with wide interests. Everybody who was anybody knew him in Williamsburg, where he sat in the House of Burgesses, Virginia's legislature. Sometimes he rode to the tiny seaport of Yorktown to check his tobacco before it went off to England. Or he'd join his friends in Philadelphia to talk politics and discuss where the colonies were heading.

Today he was returning to the Pennsylvania capital as a Virginia member of the Second Continental Congress. Martha could tell that her man was troubled. Despite the glorious day, there was a somber feeling, no, a feeling of *danger,* in the air. The world they'd known all their lives seemed to be spinning out of control. Only two weeks before, news had come of a fight outside Boston, Massachusetts. Minutemen had fired on the king's troops at Lexington and Concord. Lives had been lost on both sides and feelings were running high. The British army was now bottled up in Boston by thousands of angry men from Massachusetts and other New England colonies. There was even talk of bands of Virginia backwoodsmen, lean, tough Indian fighters, preparing to march north.

The houseboy closed the carriage door and the driver cracked his whip. George Washington wondered where it would all end. All he knew for sure was that the fighting near Boston was only the beginning of a terrible conflict— one still without a name. He also knew that he'd be drawn into it as surely as magnets attract iron; that's why he'd packed his blue and red uniform as a colonel of the Virginia militia.

We know the conflict he was heading into as the American Revolution, next to Vietnam our country's longest war. For eight years, 1775–1783, Washington would lead the rebels against the world's mightiest empire. It would be a cruel war, full of death, and pain, and hatred. Especially hatred. Naturally, much of the hatred would be directed toward the British, seen as an invader come to rob the people of their freedom. But the bitterest hatred would be against fellow Americans, since the Revolution was also our first civil war.

Thousands of Americans remained loyal to King George III, joining his forces against the rebels. Thus neighbor fought neighbor; families broke up, members sometimes killing one another.

American independence didn't come easily or cheaply. Yet, despite the odds, Washington and his Continentals— "the Ragged, Lousey, Naked regiment," one officer called them—won. Their victory created the United States of America and set its course for the future.

Americans constantly turn back to the Revolution to renew their faith in their country and its ideals. The Revolution lives in us in ways we may not recognize. Schoolyard sayings such as "It's a free country" and "Majority rules" are part of our Revolutionary heritage.

More, the American Revolution is one of the bright spots in human history. It is the first "war of national liberation," the first time common people carried out a successful rebellion and created a new nation. And that nation was special, unlike any that had ever existed.

Abraham Lincoln understood this when he came to Gettysburg, Pennsylvania, in 1863 to honor the dead of our second civil war. America, he said, is "a new nation, conceived in Liberty, and dedicated to the proposition that all men are created equal." True, that nation wasn't perfect, nor is it perfect today. For too long women, blacks, and the poor had few rights or no rights at all. What they did have, however, was the Revolution, a beacon to guide them in the right direction.

Then, as now, the Revolution challenged Americans to be true to their ideals, while encouraging the oppressed to struggle for the rights that are theirs. Then, as now, the Revolution challenged Americans to honor those who struggle for liberty and independence everywhere in the world.

# ONE

# Seeds of Revolution

*T*HE AMERICAN Revolution grew from the seeds of another conflict, the French and Indian War. Between 1755 and 1760, the French in Canada and their Indian allies fought Great Britain and her North American colonies. The war had begun unofficially in 1754, when twenty-two-year-old militia officer George Washington ambushed a French patrol in the Pennsylvania backwoods. From then on the conflict escalated quickly, spreading to Europe, where an estimated million people died.

It was rough going for the British at first. Disaster followed disaster. A powerful army under General Edward Braddock was trapped near Fort Duquesne, today's Pittsburgh, Pennsylvania, by a few hundred Indians led by French officers. Braddock died from a bullet through the lungs and, had it not been for his aide, young Washington, the whole army would have been destroyed. Indian war parties then began to strike frontier settlements. Burned cabins and rotting corpses littered the backcountry from the Canadian border to Georgia. It was a time of nightmares come true, when settlers said there was "blood on the moon."

Slowly, painfully, the British learned from their mistakes. Frontiersmen formed special units called "rangers" to bring the war home to the Indians. Rangers, led by such daring commanders as Major Robert Rogers, burned Indian villages in return and slaughtered tribesmen as they slept. The mother country sent reinforcements led by able generals like James Wolfe, a tall beanpole of a man dying from an unknown disease. Sickness, however, didn't keep Wolfe from crushing the French army on the Plains of Abraham outside the walls of Quebec city, Canada. Wolfe was killed in the battle, but his victory forced France to make peace. Britain took Canada, and France's possessions in the Ohio Valley, along with her territories in India. Thus the British Empire became the largest the world had ever known, larger even than that of the Romans.

Yet the Empire's most precious jewel remained the thirteen colonies: Massachusetts, New Hampshire, Connecticut, Rhode Island, New York, Pennsylvania, New Jersey, Delaware, Maryland, Virginia, North Carolina, South Carolina, Georgia. This fifteen-hundred-mile strip along the Atlantic seaboard was where the United States would be born.

Although settlers had been clearing the land for nearly two centuries, it would be unrecognizable to us today. Except along the coastal plain, it was a wilderness broken by tiny patches of settlement. America was a green land of rushing streams, crystal lakes, and vast, gloomy forests; sailors could smell the northern pine forests out at sea, hours before sighting land. The most dangerous animals—bear, wolf, bobcat—had nearly disappeared from the coastal areas, but the interior teemed with game. Passenger pigeons, now extinct, flew in flocks of millions, blotting out the noonday sun. Playful porpoises greeted ships in New York's Hudson River.

Some two and a half million people lived in the colonies in 1763, a half-million of whom were black slaves. Every colony had slaves, although most lived in the South. But whether free or slave, better than nine out of every ten Americans drew their living from the land as farmers.

Towns were small, of perhaps twenty to seventy families, and widely separated. Townspeople earned their living in different ways: manufacturing, shopkeeping, foreign trade, shipbuilding, fishing, law, medicine, printing. Since there weren't any good roads, travel was slow, uncomfortable, and often dangerous, especially when roads flooded and bridges washed away during the rainy season. George Washington, for example, thought himself lucky to go from Mount Vernon to Philadelphia in five days. It took three days by coach to go the ninety miles from Philadelphia to New York City in good weather. This explains why people preferred to travel by water whenever possible. It also explains why they were patient and able to take long delays in stride.

Next to London, Philadelphia, with its 40,000 people, was the largest city in the English-speaking world. New York had 20,000 people, Boston, 16,000, Charleston, South Carolina, 12,000, and Newport, Rhode Island, 11,000. American cities were quiet places where neighbor knew neighbor and few bothered to lock doors.

The thirteen colonies were good places in which to live. In Europe, where kings and nobles owned most of the land and wealth, ordinary people had little chance of improving themselves. America, however, was a new world of opportunity. Through hard work and plenty of luck, one might achieve more in a few years than all one's ancestors in the old country.

Americans were also used to governing themselves. Each colony had its own assembly, a legislative body elected by men who owned a certain amount of property. These assemblies passed laws and voted taxes as needed. Each colony also had a governor appointed by the king, who could veto any of the assembly's laws. Yet governors seldom caused trouble, for their salaries were paid by the assemblies. Either they went along with the colonists' wishes, or they whistled for their money. Governors usually swallowed their pride and cooperated.

Still, the colonies were far from independent. Parliament,

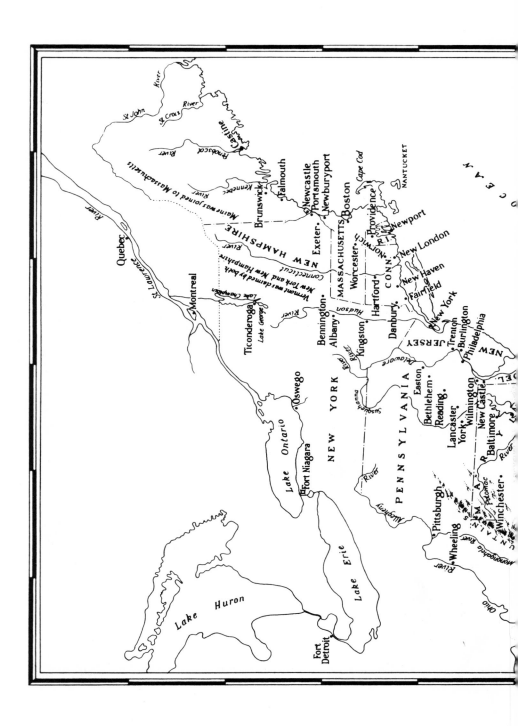

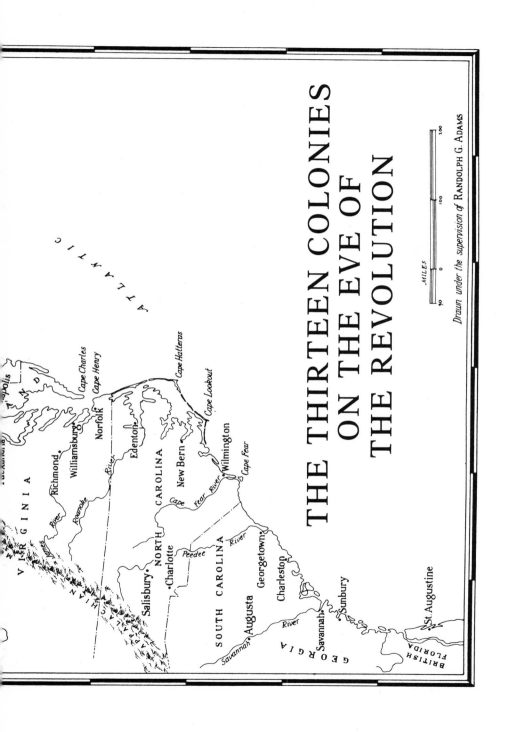

# THE THIRTEEN COLONIES ON THE EVE OF THE REVOLUTION

Drawn under the supervision of RANDOLPH G. ADAMS

MILES

ATLANTIC

VIRGINIA

Cape Charles
Cape Henry
Richmond
Williamsburg
Norfolk
Edenton
Cape Hatteras

NORTH CAROLINA
New Bern
Cape Lookout
Salisbury
Charlotte
Peedee
Cape Fear River
Wilmington
Cape Fear

SOUTH CAROLINA
Augusta
Georgetown
Charleston

GEORGIA
Savannah River
Savannah
Sunbury

BRITISH FLORIDA
St. Augustine

James River
Roanoke River

Great Britain's own lawmaking body, controlled their dealings with the outside world. Laws known as the Acts of Trade and Navigation regulated their overseas trade. Americans could sell such products as tobacco and cotton only to England, even though prices were better elsewhere. They were also forbidden to manufacture woolen cloth for sale overseas and anything else that might compete with British-made goods. Foreign products were either kept out of the colonies or taxed heavily at the seaports, forcing their prices up.

The Acts of Trade and Navigation were worse on paper than in reality. Since it was impossible for the Royal Navy to patrol the entire Atlantic coast, Americans easily evaded the laws. Smugglers sold colonial goods in the Dutch and French West Indies, and some made fortunes landing untaxed cargoes for sale in the colonies. Unlike today, when the smuggler is seen by most people as a criminal, in colonial times he was a respected member of the community who helped his neighbors get needed goods at fair prices. People dealt with "their" smuggler for years, like any dependable tradesman.

The Acts of Trade and Navigation were annoying, but not enough to undermine Americans' loyalty to the mother country. After all, they were more prosperous than the subjects of any other European nation. They were citizens of a mighty empire that allowed them self-government in nearly all matters.

THINGS BEGAN to change soon after the French and Indian War. In 1760, George III became king at the age of twenty-two. His Majesty was tall, blue-eyed, with a long nose, small chin, and thick lips. He was a decent man who wanted others to like him. He loved his wife, a German princess (said to have a face ugly enough to turn milk sour) and their fifteen children. A shy, quiet person, he enjoyed tinkering with clocks and supervising workers on his estates. He was doomed to spend the last years of his life blind and insane.

"Farmer George," as he liked to be called, believed that

*King George III in 1778. The king was a well-meaning man who believed anyone who disagreed with him was either a liar, a fool, or a traitor. He spent the last years of his life blind and insane.*

God had given him the British Empire to rule with wisdom and justice. Unfortunately, he wasn't very wise. Once an idea came into his mind, he locked onto it like a steel trap. He became so stubborn, so sure that he was right, that nothing could make him think differently. "I wish nothing but good," he'd say, "therefore everyone who does not agree with me is a traitor and a scoundrel."

George III was no dictator able to do whatever he pleased. He, like his humblest subject, had to obey the law of the land. Yet Parliament, which made the laws, didn't truly represent the English people. Fewer than one man in five could vote, and he was nearly always a landowner or businessman. Worse, no American could vote in a British election, much less represent his colony in Parliament. This meant that Americans were, in effect, ruled by strangers, people who'd never visited their country or knew about its problems firsthand.

The king, wealthier than anyone in his realm, used his money and position to influence Parliament in ways that are illegal today. Voters were bribed. Government jobs went to members of Parliament who saw things His Majesty's way. The royal estates, which included entire towns, always elected "The King's Friends." If the prime minister or other high official displeased His Majesty, even though he might be liked by the people, the king replaced him with someone he trusted.

The king trusted George Grenville, who became prime minister in 1763. Grenville faced a difficult task when he took office. The war with France had been the costliest in British history. Within eight years the national debt had nearly doubled, from 72 million pounds to 132 million pounds, worth about $30 billion in today's money. Prices skyrocketed. Hungry mobs rioted in London to force down food prices. Rioting became so serious that troops had to shoot into the crowds, for English cities had no police to keep order.

Despite Britain's victory, Prime Minister Grenville worried about the colonies. To prevent a French return, and to keep the Indians in line, he decided to station ten thousand troops permanently in the colonies. But who should pay for this army? Surely not the English, already heavily taxed. Since the Americans would benefit from military protection, it seemed only right that they should pick up the bill.

The key part of Grenville's program was the Stamp Act of 1765. Until then, the colonies had paid the mother country only import duties on foreign goods. The Stamp Act was different. It was a direct tax voted by Parliament to be collected in America. Every lawyer's license, marriage certificate, college diploma and land deed, every bill of sale, will, mortgage and newspaper, had to bear a colored stamp. An unstamped document had no value, and anyone using it would be fined by special tax courts.

The Stamp Act was the biggest mistake of Grenville's career. News of it shook the colonies like an earthquake. Americans disagreed about many things, but this united them as never before. The amount to be charged was not the problem; their own assemblies often taxed them more heavily. *Their own assemblies!* That was the point. Americans were used to *electing* those who taxed them. If they disliked the taxes, they voted the taxers out of office and elected those who'd change the law. It was that simple. No one could force the people to accept anything that a majority of the people wasn't ready to accept itself. But Americans couldn't hold members of Parliament accountable at the polls. These men, many of whom took the king's money for their votes, could order Americans about without consulting them.

Taxation without representation was tyranny in American eyes. If Parliament could tax the papers they used without their consent, it could tax anything. "Nay!" cried an angry colonist. "I don't know but that they would find means to tax you for every child you got, and for every kiss your daughters received from their sweethearts; and, God knows, that would soon ruin you." To be taxed without your consent meant that you weren't your own person. You were unfree, as much a slave as the poor soul sold on the auction block.

People vowed to resist the Stamp Act before it did harm. Some resisted with words. Delegates from nine colonies met in a Stamp Act Congress in New York City to denounce the tax. Others backed words with action, hitting the British in a tender spot, their pocketbooks. Colonists boycotted Brit-

*Colonists hated the Stamp Act. Their own version of the stamps showed they believed they were a death sentence for American liberties.*

ish products, refusing to buy anything made in the mother country. The smugglers' trade soared, while goods piled up in English warehouses and English workers became unemployed.

Not all resistance was peaceful. Groups calling themselves Sons of Liberty or Liberty Boys sprang up everywhere. Their members came from all walks of life, from roughneck dockworkers to prosperous merchants. These men put muscle behind resistance to the Stamp Act.

Sons of Liberty would visit a stamp distributor to advise him that his neighbors hoped he'd resign for his own good. To encourage him, rocks were thrown through his windows late at night; window glass was very expensive and a few broken panes were a real loss to a homeowner. He'd awaken to find human filth smeared on his front door, or his likeness hanging from a tree across the road. In New London, Connecticut, the stamp distributor's likeness was dragged through the streets to shouts of "There hangs a Traitor, there's an Enemy of his Country."

If he didn't resign, the Liberty Boys became violent. Stamp distributors' houses were pulled down and their possessions trampled in the mud. More than one terrified man was chased out of town, never to return, by a club-swinging mob. Fortunately, nobody was killed. A few stamps were sold in Georgia, but otherwise they lay unused in government offices.

Parliament saw that the Stamp Act couldn't be enforced and repealed it in 1766. America went wild with joy when the news arrived. The Boston Sons of Liberty danced through the streets and lit bonfires on Bunker Hill across the harbor. Free beer was given out in New York City and the assembly voted money for a magnificent statue of George III to stand at the foot of Broadway. During the excitement few noticed that Parliament also passed the Declaratory Act, giving itself power to make any law whatever for America. This was a dangerous step, for it meant that Parliament could override, even abolish, the colonial assemblies, thereby ending self-government in America.

Things remained quiet until the spring of 1767, when Parliament found another way to tax the colonies. The Townshend Act, named for its sponsor Charles Townshend, put heavy duties on certain English goods coming into American ports. The list included paper, paint, glass, lead, and tea. The colonists responded with another boycott.

American women played an important part in making the boycott a success. Patriotic girls calling themselves Daughters of Liberty vowed never to marry men who bought English goods. Housewives stopped serving tea, a favorite drink; they brewed coffee instead, smuggled by the shipload from the

*After the Stamp Act's repeal, the evil law was "buried" in solemn ceremonies throughout the colonies.*

Dutch West Indies. Women gave up English cloth, a real sacrifice, since the finest fabrics and clothing styles came from the mother country. They set up spinning schools in churches and held all-day spinning bees to make their own cloth. It was coarse homespun, but Americans wore it proudly as a symbol of their determination to fight for their rights.

The Sons of Liberty treated those who defied the boycott to tar and feather parties. To be tarred and feathered was no joke, but a torture that might cause crippling or death. The victim would be stripped naked, while a barrel of tar was brought to a boil before his eyes. The hissing, bubbling goo was then poured over him with a long-handled ladle or applied with a mop. A stream of black fire flowed down his neck, shoulders, chest, back, and legs. If tar got into his eyes, he screamed in terror as he went blind. A feather pillow was then torn open and emptied over him to make him look like some weird chicken. Finally, he was "ridden out of town on a rail." A wooden fence rail was slipped between his legs and lifted by a man at either end; a man stood on each side to prevent his falling off. Thus mounted, he was carried through the streets, feeling as though he'd split in half at any moment. They took him out of town and tossed him in a ditch, where he lay until someone picked him up. Removing the tar was worse than anything. The burned skin came off in strips during the following weeks, leaving him scarred for life. Some tar-and-feather victims never recovered, and went insane from their ordeal.

The Liberty Boys found after a while that the threat was as effective as the deed. All they had to do was send a person a ball of cold tar and feathers in the morning to have him leave town by afternoon.

The boycott was gaining strength when a Boston merchant named John Hancock had a run-in with the customs officers who inspected ships and collected duties on imported goods. In June 1768, customs agents seized his ship *Liberty* as a smuggler's vessel. Hancock was not only the richest man in Boston, but an outspoken foe of taxation without represen-

*A not-so-funny British cartoon entitled "The Bostonians Paying the Excise-Man, or, Tarring and Feathering." In addition to an outfit of tar and feathers, this tax collector was forced to drink a pot of boiling tea.*

tation. As soon as the *Liberty* was taken, a crowd marched to the waterfront. The customs agents were beaten up and chased aboard a British warship anchored in the harbor.

Boycotts. Defiance. Housewrecking. Tar and feather parties. And now assaulting His Majesty's customs agents! That was the last straw. The British government decided to send troops to keep order in Boston.

AT THREE O'CLOCK in the afternoon of September 30, 1768, a squadron of warships dropped anchor in Boston Harbor. People who'd climbed the rooftops for a better view could tell that their captains were taking no chances. The vessels lay broadside to the town with open gunports. Any resistance would meet a storm of fire and iron.

Next morning, seven hundred Redcoats clambered ashore at the Long Wharf. Forming ranks, they marched through town with loaded muskets, fixed bayonets, drums beating and fifes tootling. From the moment they pitched their tents on Boston Common, the time bomb of revolution began to tick.

The Redcoats were very different from the Bostonians, who saw them as invaders come to enforce unjust laws. Americans were not strangers to military service. Each colony required able-bodied men between sixteen and sixty-five to belong to the militia. The militiaman was a citizen-soldier, a part-time warrior who owned his own musket, usually kept on the wall near the kitchen fireplace. Several times each year, militia companies drilled on the village green to keep up their skills. Officers were respectful of their men, for each company elected its own officers. Since officers and men were neighbors, they did without formalities such as saluting and called each other by their first names. If war came, they served for a few weeks or months, depending upon their agreement with the colonial government. But war or no war, when a company's time expired, everyone went home unless he reenlisted of his own free will.

There was nothing free about the Redcoats, who seemed

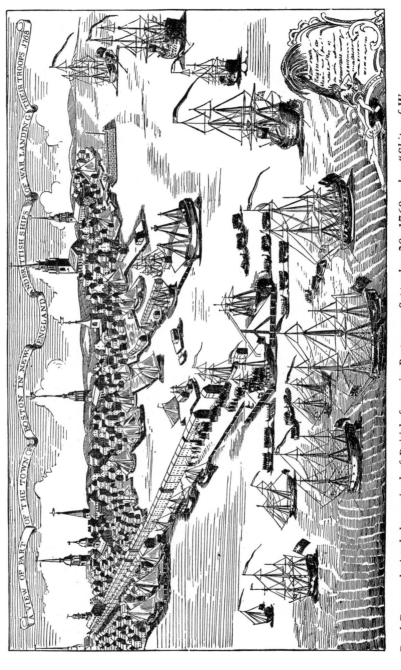

Paul Revere depicted the arrival of British forces in Boston on September 30, 1768, when "Ships of War, armed Schooners, Transports, etc., came up the Harbour and Anchored round the Town; their Cannon Loaded."

like slaves in gaudy uniforms. These men were "regulars," professional soldiers who formed Great Britain's standing army. For them, the army wasn't just a career, but home, family, a way of life.

The British army was officered by gentlemen who'd done little, if anything, to earn high rank. In the days of George III, officers' commissions were sold to the highest bidder, a practice that continued until 1871. Since army commissions were good investments, men gladly bought them for themselves or their children. As a result, colonels of regiments might be babies in diapers. Boys of sixteen often led full-grown men into battle. Money, not merit, decided promotion. A wealthy idiot easily rose in the service, while another man, able but poor, remained a captain for life.

The Redcoat, or common soldier, was feared by friend and enemy alike. Respectable families would sooner see a son dead than "gone for a soldier." Soldiering was a low, nasty profession. No one enlisted unless he had to. England's dropouts, no-goods, and failures enlisted as a last resort to fill empty bellies. Whole regiments were made up of convicts and men marked for death. Not that these were murderers, who were always hung. There were two hundred offenses that carried the death penalty, ranging from treason to pickpocketing a silk handkerchief. Judges often gave prisoners a choice between the army or the noose. Enlistment was for life, or until a man became too old or sick to serve.

The regular's life was a never-ending routine of discomfort, drudgery, and discipline. Discomfort began with the uniform, the same in all seasons; winter or summer, soldiers dressed in heavy, itchy wool that fit tight as a straitjacket. A Redcoat wore just that—a scarlet overcoat with colorful linings, piping, lace, and buttons of brass or pewter. Beneath the coat he wore a waistcoat, a long vest of red or white linen, depending on his regiment. To make him stand straight, a stiff leather collar was placed under the chin, which rubbed his neck raw in hot weather. He also wore white knee breeches so tight that they had to be put on wet, cutting off blood circulation in the legs when they dried. Boots and long, buttoned gaiters came up over the knee. Crisscrossed belts for the bayonet and cartridge box formed a perfect *X* over his chest. Hats were of heavy bearskin or tall brass helmets, brimless, so that the sun glared in his eyes. Officers felt that discomfort made their men ferocious when turned loose on the enemy.

The Redcoat on the march was a beast of burden who carried nearly his own weight on his back. Standard gear was a fourteen-pound musket, a one-pound bayonet, a pound or two of musket balls, a shovel, and a knapsack full of extra clothing, food, blanket, personal items, and tenting equipment. This load weighed 120 to 125 pounds, compared to the 60-pound pack carried by American infantrymen today. King George's troops wore their knapsacks in battle, while modern soldiers usually put them aside or toss them into trucks.

A Redcoat needed three hours to dress and groom himself each morning, even on the morning of battle. His uniform had to be brushed spotless. Everything white—gaiters, belts, piping, lace—was kept snow-white with pipe clay. "Spit and polish" put a shine on boots, buttons, and buckles. Soldiers also had to be expert hairdressers. Combing the hair neatly wasn't enough. To pass inspection, they had to wear stiff curls on either side of the face and a long pigtail dangling behind. Curls and pigtail were plastered with the end of a tallow candle and powdered with flour. Unwashed hair attracted flies in summer and stank the year round. Redcoats had to be cleanshaven, without beards or mustaches.

A private earned eight pence a day, about two cents in American money. Before he saw his pay, however, there were "stoppages," deductions for shoes, socks, gloves, medicine, repairing his musket, and other expenses that came out of his own pocket. The remainder—if any—never met his needs, especially if he had a family.

A married soldier often brought his family with him. Redcoats' wives were entitled to army rations in return for serving as "necessary women" who cooked, washed, and nursed the wounded; children drew quarter-rations. Several regiments had as many women and children as fighting men. There was no such thing as privacy. In barracks, a blanket hung on a rope separated the soldier and his family from his snoring comrades. When the army moved, so did wives and youngsters, sharing all the hardships of the march and the dangers of battle. Army children learned the facts of life early and got used to the sight of blood.

Wherever they were stationed, Redcoats tried to make ends meet by doing odd jobs in off-duty hours. Men in full uniform were to be seen digging ditches, plowing fields, chopping wood, and driving wagons. They were often great thieves, and their wives and children too, stealing anything that wasn't nailed down. No wonder townspeople dreaded their coming. English towns often had crude signs warning "No dogs or soldiers allowed."

Army discipline was savage. Redcoats were treated not as reasoning human beings, but as dumb brutes to be driven by fear. Breaking the slightest rule meant the "cat," or cat-o'-nine-tails, a whip of nine knotted cords fastened to a handle. An offender was whipped as many as a thousand times on his bare back. If he screamed, a stick was shoved between his teeth. If he fainted, a bucket of salt water on the bleeding wounds revived him fast enough. Other men ran the gauntlet; that is, they had to dash between two lines of soldiers who'd beat them with sticks every inch of the way.

Serious offenses such as desertion and murder meant death. One reason for dressing soldiers in red was to make them easily identifiable if they ran away. Another was that red hid blood stains, preventing panic when someone was hit in the closely packed ranks during battle. The worst punishment, however, wasn't death, but "removing aboard a frigate," transfer to a warship. Even the most hardened Redcoat trembled at the thought of naval discipline.

BOSTONIANS were horrified at seeing men's backs torn open with the cat; doubly so at seeing a private standing on the Common, next to his coffin, waiting to be shot in the head. Such cruelties made them more determined than ever to go ahead with the boycott on English goods. They felt that if they allowed themselves to be wrongfully taxed, there'd come a time when *they'd* be treated like Redcoats.

The Redcoats themselves annoyed people no end. Common folks—laborers, dockworkers, the unemployed—resented their competition for low-paying jobs. Bostonians also had families, and it wasn't fair that they should suffer because the king paid his troops so badly.

More serious was the soldiers' deliberate nastiness, especially on Sundays. Bostonians, like their Puritan ancestors, took religion seriously, and their churches were always filled on the Sabbath. It was then that officers raced horses on the Common, gambled, and paraded bands under church windows.

Off-duty privates got drunk and serenaded churchgoers with "Yankee Doodle." A folksong first heard during the French and Indian War, "Yankee Doodle" made fun of the New England militia serving near Fort Ticonderoga in New York. Everyone knew some of its hundreds of verses. The most famous verses were:

> *Yankee Doodle came to town*
> *A-riding on a pony,*
> *He stuck a feather in his hat*
> *And called it macaroni.*

> *Yankee Doodle keep it up,*
> *Yankee Doodle Dandy,*
> *Mind the music and the step*
> *and with the girls be handy.*

This catchy song caused bloody noses and split lips. "To yankie" was Scottish slang for tricking someone or making an unfair bargain. New Englanders, being good businessmen, were mocked as "Yankees." "Doodle" is slang for fool. "Macaroni" refers to the Italian food introduced into London in the 1750s. Some Londoners were following a fad for anything Italian and were macaroni addicts, not only serving it with every meal, but wearing queer "macaroni clothes" and inventing silly "macaroni manners." Thus, in "Yankee Doodle," New Englanders were dishonest, overdressed fools. American rebels would later take over the song and fling it in the Redcoats' teeth as a sign of defiance. But for the time being, it angered Bostonians.

People struck back. Youngsters threw stones, shouting "Bloodybacks!" as they ran away. Liberty Boys pelted soldiers with garbage or rushed up from behind and pushed them face down into the mud. "Lobsterbacks," people cried. "Lobsters . . . Lo-obsters for sale!" This word had a double meaning. It referred to the regulars' red coat and to the lobster, whose shell turns red in boiling; lobster was also so plentiful in colonial times that it was fed to slaves instead of the costlier bread. Shouting matches, pushing incidents, and fistfights happened daily in Boston. Everybody knew that people would die sooner or later. The only questions were who and when.

The answers came on a raw, dreary night, Monday, March 5, 1770. A layer of ice and frozen mud lay on the ground, covered by several inches of fresh snow. It was dark, and since Boston had no streetlamps, the only light came from the moon's reflection off the snow. Groups of men, mostly rough-looking types, stood about. Occasionally passersby heard the word "lobster," followed by guffaws and curses.

Private Hugh White stood guard in King Street at the Custom House, where ship captains came to pay the duties on their cargoes. The soldier stood straight as a rail, his musket resting on his left shoulder, thinking whatever bored sentries think on lonely nights. But his boredom didn't last long.

At about eight o'clock an officer he knew passed on an errand. As the officer, a captain, crossed King Street near the sentry post, Edward Garrick, a teenaged barber's helper, called out that the captain hadn't paid his barber bill. The captain ignored him and went about his business.

Not Private Hugh White. Stepping from his post, he insisted, loudly, that the captain was a gentleman who always paid his bills. Garrick, just as loudly, said there weren't any gentlemen in the British army. Quick as a wink, White whacked him with the butt of his musket, sending him skidding into the gutter. The boy howled in pain and ran away. The soldier returned to his post.

Garrick returned minutes later with a group of young men. Having friends with him made him brave, and he began to curse the soldier. "Lousy rascal!" he shouted. "Damned rascally scoundrel lobster!" Others took up the cry, attracting men from the nearby docks. By now at least fifty men stood in front of Private White, the crowd growing by the minute. "Kill the soldier!" they shouted. "Kill the damned coward, kill him, knock him down!" We know their words from the testimony bystanders later gave in court.

Snowballs packed around stones, jagged clam shells, and fist-sized chunks of ice began to fly toward White's head. This was no boys' lark, but an assault that could easily have crippled the soldier. Terrified, he retreated up the Custom House steps. He pounded on the door with his fist, but there was no one to let him in. "Turn out the main guard!" he cried. His cry reached the nearby barracks, where Captain Thomas Preston was officer of the day. Preston took seven men and rushed out the door, buckling on his sword as he went.

At that very moment a mysterious man had just finished supper at a local tavern. In his late forties, barrel-chested, he stood six feet two inches tall—a giant for those days. People knew him by two names: Michael Johnson and Crispus Attucks. He may have been a black ex-slave, or an Indian, or a mixture of the two; no one can be sure today. Little is known about him except that he worked on the docks and died violently.

Hearing the hubbub, the big man set out with thirty

sailor friends to join the action. Each carried a heavy club. They were looking for trouble, and they found it.

They arrived as Captain Preston's squad was moving through the crowd behind lowered bayonets. Joining Private White, the squad faced the crowd, now grown to over three hundred. "Why do you not fire?" voices called. "Damn you, you dare not fire! Fire and be damned!" The crowd was not being brave in daring the Redcoats to shoot. Everyone knew that soldiers couldn't open fire in peacetime without an order from the civilian government, and that doing so was a hanging offense. By shouting as it did, the crowd was simply feeding its own "courage" while frightening the soldiers.

Preston stepped in front of his men to reason with the crowd. It was useless. As he spoke, Crispus Attucks struck his arm with his club, paralyzing it for several minutes. The big man then turned and hit a soldier over the head, knocking *him* down and his musket from his hands.

King Street was a madhouse. Sailors rapping clubs on musket barrels. Redcoats pale with terror. Shouts. Curses. Taunts. Threats.

"Kill the lobsters! Kill them! Kill them! Kill! Kill! Kill!"

"Why do you not fire? Fire! Fire! Fire!"

Shots rang out.

The soldiers, confused and afraid they were about to be murdered, opened fire without orders. They fired singly, each man on his own, not in a coordinated volley. But their bullets easily found marks in the surging crowd. When the smoke cleared, five men lay dead or dying. Among the bodies was Crispus Attucks with two bullets in his chest. Blood mingled with the fresh snow and the frozen mud of King Street.

Captain Preston and his men were charged with murder and held for trial. It looked grim for the Redcoats, since few expected a Boston jury to find them innocent.

One day a friend of Preston's came to John Adams in tears, begging him to lead the soldiers' defense. Adams was a potbellied little man with rosy cheeks and a razor-sharp

*John Adams defended the soldiers charged with the "Boston Massacre" even though he believed the colonies might have to fight a bloody war to win their independence. Painting by Charles Willson Peale.*

mind. He was one of the best lawyers in Boston. While most colonists still wanted to live peacefully as British subjects, Adams believed the colonies must be independent even at the cost of a bloody war. Years later he'd become the second president of the United States. Above all, though, John Adams believed in justice. Like his neighbors, he resented the Red-coats. Even so, they were due a fair trial, and he'd see that they got it no matter what happened to him personally.

Fellow Bostonians let Adams know how they felt about his defending redcoated "murderers." Some threw mud. Voices whispered from shadows, "Who buys lobsters, John Adams?" He came home one night to find a window broken. Abigail, his wife, held out two stones she'd picked up from the floor. "They are only small stones," she said. "That is why I kept them to show you. You must not fear to leave me."

Adams swallowed his anger and went to work. During the trial he argued that the soldiers weren't guilty of murder, but had fired in self-defense. The mob outside the Custom House was attacking the soldiers. What were they supposed to do? Wait to be killed? That is not reasonable; no one can expect a person to allow himself to be killed. The jury— a Boston jury—agreed. The soldiers were found innocent of murder and freed. "God bless you, Mr. Adams," they said, tears rolling down their cheeks.

The trial ended, but the memory of the shooting was kept alive by two men: Samuel Adams and Paul Revere. Sam Adams, shabbily dressed, his hands shaking and lips twitching, was known to everyone in Boston. He was a dear man, generous to all in need, even if little money remained for his own family. Like his cousin John, he believed the colonies must be independent. But unlike his cousin, he had an inborn gift for stirring up people. Sam would have done anything to make life miserable for the British. He had orga-nized the Boston Sons of Liberty and would create the Com-mittees of Correspondence to keep patriots in all colonies in-formed of Britain's misdeeds. In his pamphlets he invented the "Boston Massacre," turning a riot into a deliberate slaugh-ter of innocent patriots. He saw to it that, for years afterward, the Boston Massacre was remembered in "hate Britain" speeches and parades not only in Massachusetts, but in the other colonies.

*Paul Revere's drawing of "The Bloody Massacre" in Boston. The picture contains more propaganda than truth. Notice that he renamed the Custom House "Butcher's Hall," that the citizens are unarmed, and that the soldiers are firing on their captain's command.*

Sam's friend, Paul Revere, was an engraver and silversmith whose works are now prized by museums. Revere engraved the famous picture of Captain Preston, his sword raised and an evil grin on his face, ordering the Redcoats to fire into the "peaceful" crowd. Behind the soldiers is the Custom House, renamed Butcher's Hall. The picture carried a poem calling upon people to remember their slain heroes:

> *Unhappy Boston, see thy sons deplore,*
> *Thy hallow'd Walks besmeared with guiltless Gore.*

They did remember. For years Revere's picture of the Boston Massacre hung in American homes. Generations of youngsters learned history from the artist's most famous work.

THE BRITISH tried to calm things down after the Boston Massacre. At the end of March 1770, the troops were sent from town to Castle William, a fortress on an island in the harbor. In April, the Townshend Act was repealed except for the tax on tea, which was kept to show that Parliament still had the right to tax the colonies. The colonists' boycott ended as well, on everything but tea, which Americans either refused to drink or bought from smugglers.

The next outburst took Britain completely by surprise. The king's new prime minister was Frederick, Lord North. A jolly, easygoing fellow, Lord North often fell asleep during debates in Parliament. When he'd awaken and hear everyone laughing, he joined in, although the joke was often on him. Yet he was a skilled politician who'd hold office for twelve years, longer than any other of George III's ministers.

Lord North's greatest problem was that he knew little about America and Americans. He meant well; he surely didn't want war, but ignorance led him to make a dangerous error. At first that error seemed like a good idea. The East India Company had a monopoly on importing tea into Britain, although not of selling it in the colonies. Tea arriving from Asia was auctioned to London merchants, who then sold it to American merchants for sale in the colonies. The continuing boycott, however, caused seventeen million pounds of tea to pile up in London warehouses, with more pouring in daily.

The East India Company faced bankruptcy. Its shareholders, many of them nobles and merchants with political influence, protested. Members of Parliament, several of whom were on the company's board of directors, told Lord North of their concern. The bankruptcy of such a company would have been a national disaster, like the failure of a giant corporation today.

Lord North had a simple answer to the East India Company's problems: extend its monopoly to the colonies. The company would send tea directly to American agents, who'd pay the tax, which they'd add to the price consumers paid. Everyone—or nearly everyone—would gain, he believed. The East India Company would be saved, and its powerful backers made happy. Despite the tea tax, elimination of English and American middlemen would allow the price to fall to an all-time low. Low prices would drive away Dutch smugglers. American troublemakers like John Hancock would lose profits. And the colonists? No problem, according to His Lordship. Americans knew a good thing and would forget that "nonsense" about taxation without representation for the sake of a cheap cup of tea.

By trying to help the East India Company, Lord North triggered the American Revolution. Americans were not as gullible as he thought. They knew that the price of tea would rise once the smugglers were driven out of business. Worse, they saw the lower price as a back door to tyranny, a way of breaking the boycott and with it the colonists' will to resist. If that happened, the British would be able to do anything they pleased.

Americans vowed to resist Lord North's plan. In New York and Philadelphia, tea ships were turned away by grim-faced crowds with clubs and paving stones torn from the streets. The tea unloaded at Charleston, South Carolina, was stored in a damp warehouse, where it spoiled.

Boston gave a tea party. When three tea ships—*Dartmouth, Eleanor,* and *Beaver*—anchored at Griffin's Wharf, Sons of Liberty mounted a guard, not to protect the cargo, but to keep it from being taken ashore. On December 16, 1773, five thousand people crowded into and around the Old South Meeting House to hear Sam Adams demand that the ships leave—or else. As the meeting broke up, there were shouts of "The Mohawks are come!" and "Boston Harbor a teapot tonight!" Sam had seen to every detail and his "Mohawks," all trusted Liberty Boys, knew their jobs.

*Feathered "Mohawks" make saltwater tea during the Boston Tea Party.*

At about 9 P.M. two hundred men marched to the waterfront two by two. They were the strangest sight Bostonians had seen in a long time. Each man carried an axe, or "tommyhawk," over his shoulder and did odd dance steps along the way. Each wore a blanket Indian-style around his waist and feathers in his cap. Each face was painted red or blackened with chimney soot.

The phony Mohawks marched to the tea ships, where the Liberty Boys stepped aside to let them aboard. The ships' crews were told to keep out of the way; the Mohawks' business wasn't with them, but with the cargo belowdecks. Sailors, thinking tea chests not worth a broken head, didn't interfere.

The raiders went to work, using the ships' cranes to hoist the heavy chests on deck. In all, 342 chests were broken open and thrown into the harbor with their contents to make "saltwater tea." Before leaving, each man had to open his coat to show that he hadn't stolen any tea; after all, they were patriots, not pirates. One fellow had filled the lining of his coat with tea leaves. He was stripped naked, given a mud bath, and sent away black and blue.

Children always remembered their fathers coming home that night with painted faces. Later they told their own children how an "Indian" grandpa looked down on them in bed.

News of the Boston tea party spread like wildfire. Men raised wine glasses in taverns from Massachusetts to Georgia to sing the latest song:

> *Rally Mohawks! Bring out your axes.*
> *Let's tell King George we'll pay no taxes*
> *On his foreign tea.*

The British weren't amused. Sam Adams had backed the government into a corner. Either it stood firm, or it would be shamed in the eyes of the world. "The die is now cast," George III wrote Lord North. "The colonies must either submit or triumph."

Parliament passed three Coercive or "Intolerable" Acts aimed at Massachusetts. The Massachusetts Government Act ended self-government in the colony. The Quartering Act allowed the army to take over private buildings for barracks; the Redcoats were returning, and this time they'd stay. The Boston Port Act closed Boston Harbor until its citizens paid for the ruined tea. Boston was blockaded, forbidden to trade overseas, or even to send a ferry across its own harbor. This law was Boston's death sentence. The town lived by seafaring. If its sailors, merchants, and fishermen couldn't put to sea, its shipbuilders, dockers, and shopkeepers would starve. That was a high price to pay for saltwater tea.

The king chose Lieutenant General Thomas Gage to enforce the Intolerable Acts. "Tommy" Gage was an experienced officer who'd served in America since the French and Indian War. He, like George Washington, had been with General Braddock at Fort Duquesne.

Gage arrived in Boston with four thousand Redcoats May 14, 1774, in a howling rainstorm. But the weather was pleasant, compared to his reception. Although he was chief of His Majesty's forces in America and Massachusetts's new governor, the Bostonians were unimpressed. These stubborn Yankee Doodles made it clear that, whatever he did, they'd never pay for the tea. Never!

Their determination was strengthened by the other colonies. The Intolerable Acts were an alarm bell for all Americans. What was happening to Boston might happen to any town. Boston was suffering for American rights and deserved American support.

Help arrived from every colony. Cattle, sheep, hogs, fish, and grain were sent to Salem and Marblehead by sea and loaded on wagons for the overland haul to Boston. From the distant Waxhaws, the frontier area between North and South Carolina, came beef and barley. The master of Mount Vernon offered his help: "I will raise 1000 Men, subsist them at my own Expense, and march my self at their Head for the relief of Boston." The town's spirits rose, for the people knew they weren't alone.

Virginia now began to take a larger part in the struggle. When the governor dissolved the House of Burgesses for voting to aid Boston, members refused to disband. They met instead at the Raleigh Tavern in Williamsburg and voted to call a Continental Congress to discuss the colonies' grievances and to plan action. Everywhere patriots held special conventions to elect delegates to the Continental Congress. Fifty-four delegates represented every colony except Georgia. Virginia and Massachusetts sent two future presidents of the United States: George Washington and John Adams. Sam Adams was there to remind members to resist British tyranny.

The Continental Congress opened in Carpenters' Hall, Philadelphia, September 5, 1774. Delegates denounced the Intolerable Acts and voted to renew the boycott against all British goods. The boycott was called The Association and had special Committees of Inspection in each community to see that it was obeyed. These committees were an American secret police. They poked into everyone's business, and God help those caught selling British-made goods or drinking East India Company tea. Once again tar bubbled, feathers flew, and men were ridden out of town on rails.

Members of the Continental Congress hoped Lord North would see reason and repeal the Intolerable Acts before it was too late. A Second Continental Congress was called for May 1775, to discuss the colonies' next moves.

Time for a peaceful settlement was running out quickly. Even as delegates were voting in Carpenters' Hall, Massachusetts's Sons of Liberty were preparing for the worst—war. There was no telling what General Gage might do, so they had to be ready for anything. Members of each village militia company volunteered as Minutemen, promising to be ready for action at a minute's notice. Each Minuteman equipped himself with a soldier's basic kit: musket, powder horn, bullet mold, blanket, knapsack. Uniforms were of plain homespun. At least twice a week, daily in some places, Minutemen practiced marching and quick-loading their weapons. There was no target practice because of the scarcity of gunpowder.

*Samuel Adams helped organize the Sons of Liberty and Committees of Correspondence to resist taxation without representation. From a portrait by John Singleton Copley.*

Life began to change. Village greens echoed to drum rolls and militia officers bawling commands. Boys changed their games. Hunting Indians was no longer popular; boys now played at shooting Redcoats with broomstick-muskets.

Their fathers drilled with their own weapons, mostly hunting pieces and relics of the French and Indian War, or with guns gotten illegally. Smugglers brought cargoes of gunpowder from the West Indies. Benjamin Franklin, the Pennsylvania colony's agent in London, organized a gun-running ring in the British capital. Many Englishmen favored the American cause and were willing to help with money and in other ways.

The British army in Boston also helped. Privates, always needing money, sold their weapons and reported them stolen. A cheaper way was for a patriot to treat a Redcoat to whiskey, get him drunk, and walk off with his gear.

General Gage's officers knew what was going on and tried to stop it. A farmer named Ditson was caught trying to buy a soldier's musket. Ditson was tarred and feathered and paraded through Boston with a sign around his neck: AMERICAN LIBERTY OR A SPECIMEN OF DEMOCRACY. A soldier caught selling his musket was whipped until his back resembled raw hamburger.

Paul Revere proved as good at undercover work as engraving. Revere led a gang that specialized in stealing cannon from under the soldiers' noses. An entire battery of coast-defense guns was stolen from Charlestown, across the harbor from Boston, and hidden in the country. One of the largest pieces was renamed for Sam Adams. Revere's men even burglarized a warehouse where cannon were stored, smuggling them out of town in wooden crates.

The Revere gang also went in for sabotage, ruining whatever couldn't be carried away. Wagonloads of hay for British cavalry horses tipped over in the mud. Boatloads of bricks for repairing the harbor forts sank for no apparent reason. Patriots stole cannon from Boston's North Battery and dumped them into a millpond. How they took them past the guards remains a mystery.

General Gage tried to stop the stockpiling of weapons. In February 1775, he learned that the patriots had some cannon and gunpowder at Salem. On the twenty-sixth, a Sunday, he sent troops to seize the weapons. All went well until the troops found the drawbridge raised at Northfields

*Portrait of Paul Revere by American painter John Singleton Copley.
Revere was not only a patriot, but an artist of distinction. As a
silversmith, his work was in great demand in the colonies, as it is in
museum collections today. His drawings helped incite American anger
against the mother country at the time of the Boston Tea Party.*

along their line of march to Salem. A swarm of angry Minutemen were waiting for them on the other side. Colonel Leslie, the British commander, threatened to open fire if they didn't lower the bridge instantly. The Minutemen replied with shouts of "Soldiers, redjackets, lobstercoats, cowards, *damnation to your government!*"

Fingers moved to triggers, and there would have been bloodshed, had a local minister not interfered. The regulars, he knew, couldn't back down in the face of these farmers, while the farmers meant to hold their ground no matter what happened. To allow everyone to save face, he persuaded the Minutemen to lower the bridge and Colonel Leslie to march over it and back. Leslie's pride was saved, but he had to return to Boston empty-handed.

A month after this incident, March 23, 1775, George Washington's friend Patrick Henry stood to speak at a meeting in St. John's Church, in Richmond, Virginia. Henry, a famous lawyer, urged Virginians to follow Massachusetts's lead in preparing for defense. The time for talk had passed, he said. His words rang through the white-steepled building. "We have done everything that could be done to avert the storm that is coming on. . . . Gentlemen may cry, 'Peace! peace!'— but there is no peace. The war is actually begun! The next gale that sweeps from the north will bring to our ears the clash of resounding arms! . . . Is life so dear, or peace so sweet, as to be purchased at the price of chains and slavery? Forbid it, Almighty God! I know not what course others may take; but as for me, give me liberty or give me death!"

There would be plenty of that—death—soon enough.

---

# TWO

# Shots Heard Round the World

*G*ENERAL Thomas Gage
awoke before dawn one *   * morning early in April 1775
and went to his office in Province House overlooking Boston
Harbor. He paced back and forth, his hands clasped behind
his back, deep in thought.

There was a lot to think about. On the desk lay reports
from spies, "good" Yankees loyal to their king. Their reports
detailed, among other things, the movements of John Hancock and Sam Adams. Both were preparing to attend the
Second Continental Congress and would be staying with Hancock's relative, the Reverend Jonas Clark, at Lexington, a
village twelve miles northwest of Boston. Five miles up the
road, at Concord, patriots had stored enough supplies for a
small army: muskets and cannon, barrels of gunpowder and
bullets, tents, medicines, food, entrenching tools.

Gage made his plans carefully, telling as few people as
possible of his intentions. On the eighteenth of April, Redcoats would be rowed across Boston Harbor under cover of

darkness for a raid to capture the patriot leaders and destroy their supplies. With one swift blow Gage would smash the rebellion before it began.

Secrecy was the key to success. Company commanders were ordered to have their men ready to march at a moment's notice, but not told when or what their mission would be. Sailors quietly beached longboats from the warships for repairs.

Only the top commanders knew Gage's plan. Lieutenant-Colonel Francis Smith, overweight and red-faced, would lead the strike force of eight hundred handpicked troops, grenadiers and light infantry. (Each British regiment had, in addition to regular foot soldiers, companies of special troops. Grenadiers were big, powerful men used for heavy fighting at close quarters. Light infantry were smaller, more nimble men used for patrols and to protect the flanks, or sides, of a marching regiment.) Smith's second in command was Major John Pitcairn of the Royal Marines. Known for his bad language and kind heart, Pitcairn was loved by the troops; a true professional, he hated unnecessary violence. A thousand-man reserve under Lord Hugh Percy, an experienced battlefield commander, stood by in case the main force needed help.

As time for the operation neared, Boston was sealed off from the mainland to prevent the secret from leaking. Boston in 1775 was built on a tadpole-shaped peninsula jutting into the harbor. Boston Neck, the strip connecting the peninsula to the mainland, was the long, narrow tadpole's "tail." The area around the neck was filled in during the nineteenth century. Two other peninsulas, Charlestown and Dorchester, lay north and south of the town, also joined to the mainland by narrow necks. Gage closed the road across Boston Neck and sent roving patrols into the countryside to halt travelers. Warships in the harbor were to stop any boats heading toward Charlestown. The general expected victory in a sudden controlled action with little if any loss of life. What he got was quite different.

Despite Gage's precautions, it was impossible to keep

secrets in Boston. In addition to the Sons of Liberty, whose men watched every barrack and dock, the town swarmed with self-appointed spies. Men and women, boys and girls, were constantly on the lookout for clues to Gage's next move. In the days before the raid, odd bits of information began to accumulate. A stableboy overheard officers boast about settling scores with the Yankees. A washerwoman noticed sailors patching longboats. A Redcoat's wife who worked as a maid told her mistress that her husband's grenadier company had been put on alert. This information was reported to Doctor Joseph Warren, a popular physician and a leader of the Sons of Liberty. Doctor Warren didn't know what Gage had in mind, but he could make a shrewd guess.

Doctor Warren sent a warning to the Concord patriots, who took most of the supplies out of town, hiding them under straw in barns or burying them in freshly plowed fields. He also asked Paul Revere and William Dawes, a shoemaker, to "alarum the countryside," call out the Minutemen, when the Redcoats marched.

Revere, a cautious man, wanted to make sure the alarm was given even if he and Dawes failed to get through. He contacted the Charlestown Sons of Liberty and told them to have someone watching the steeple of Boston's Old North Church every night. If the Redcoats left by way of Boston Neck, he'd have one lantern hung in the steeple for a few minutes; longer than that would alert lookouts on the warships. Two lanterns meant the Redcoats were being rowed across the harbor to the eastern bank of the Charles River.

The Redcoats turned in early on the night of April 18, a Tuesday. At nine o'clock, sergeants put their hands over the mouth of each man and whispered for him to get ready. Quietly, without lighting a candle, they slipped out of barracks and through the darkened streets to Boston Common. The only sound was of boots scraping on cobblestones. A barking dog was silenced with a bayonet. Within an hour the boats cast off and vanished into the gloom.

Yet all these precautions were in vain. As the troops

marched to their boats, Sons of Liberty were reporting to Doctor Warren, who sent word for the messengers to get moving. Dawes was soon riding over Boston Neck. Avoiding a roadblock, he turned his horse's head toward Lexington and dug his spurs into its sides.

Revere, meantime, sent a friend to hoist two lanterns and went with two other friends to a rowboat he'd hidden on the beach. As they moved through town, he remembered that he hadn't brought anything to muffle the sound of the oars. No problem. One of his companions knew a girl who lived nearby. A soft whistle and a window opened. A few whispered words and a flannel petticoat came fluttering down. Revere later told his children that the petticoat was warm when he caught it.

Arriving safely at Charlestown, Revere borrowed a horse from a Liberty Boy and set out on his great adventure. He rode out of town and, passing Breed's Hill and Bunker Hill on the right, made for Charlestown Neck. A full moon hung in the sky, a golden saucer that made the trees cast long, ghostly shadows. Suddenly the blood seemed to freeze in his veins. Looming up before him was a horrible sight. There, in the moonlight, he saw a mummified body wrapped in chains, tarred, and standing in a cage suspended from a gallows. It was the body of Mark, a slave hung for poisoning his master. His remains had hung there for twenty years as a warning to would-be lawbreakers.

And now he, Paul Revere, was riding on an errand of treason, the worst crime a subject could commit against his king. He knew the penalty. English law commanded that a traitor be hung, taken down before he died, and his intestines cut out and burned before his eyes. He was then beheaded, his body cut in quarters, and the pieces stuck on spikes for all to see.

Revere rode faster along the Lexington road. Wherever he saw a glow in the window of a house, he shouted, "The regulars are out!" He dismounted outside darkened houses to throw a handful of gravel at the windows; then, shouting, remounted and continued his journey.

It was like tossing a stone into a still pond, sending ripples in ever-widening circles from the center. Wherever Revere passed, the quiet was shattered by the *rap-tap-tap* of drums and the clang of churchbells. Minutemen tumbled out of featherbeds, grabbed muskets, and ran into the cold night. Others swung into saddles to spread the alarm further.

Revere rode up to the Reverend Clark's house in Lexington, only to have guards tell him not to make so much noise. "Noise!" he bellowed. "You'll have noise enough before long. The regulars are coming out!" Just then John Hancock opened a window. "Come in, Revere," he said. "We are not afraid of *you!*"

But Revere could stay only long enough to give his news. Dawes, who'd taken the longer route, galloped into town a few minutes later. As they rode out of town, they met Doctor Samuel Prescott of Concord. The doctor, a well-known patriot, had been courting a local girl and was on his way home.

The three were riding to alert Concord when a British cavalry patrol appeared. Instantly they scattered. The doctor jumped his horse over a stone fence and galloped up the road. Dawes fell off his horse and escaped into the woods. Revere, however, wasn't fast enough. The cavalrymen held him for a while and, after threatening to blow out his brains, did nothing more than take his horse. Thus Paul Revere's famous ride ended, not with clattering hoofbeats, but on foot along a moonlit country lane. It was 1 A.M., Wednesday, April 19, 1775.

At that moment the Redcoats' adventure was only just beginning. Everything went wrong. Their heavily loaded boats couldn't make the shore, forcing the soldiers to drop over the sides and wade the rest of the way waist-deep in water and muck. They were miserable—cold, wet, and worried. As they formed columns, the breeze brought the sound of distant churchbells. Soldiers looked at each other without speaking. Words weren't needed, for whatever their mission, they'd lost the element of surprise. Instead of turning back, Colonel Smith sent for Lord Percy's reserve and began the march to Lexington.

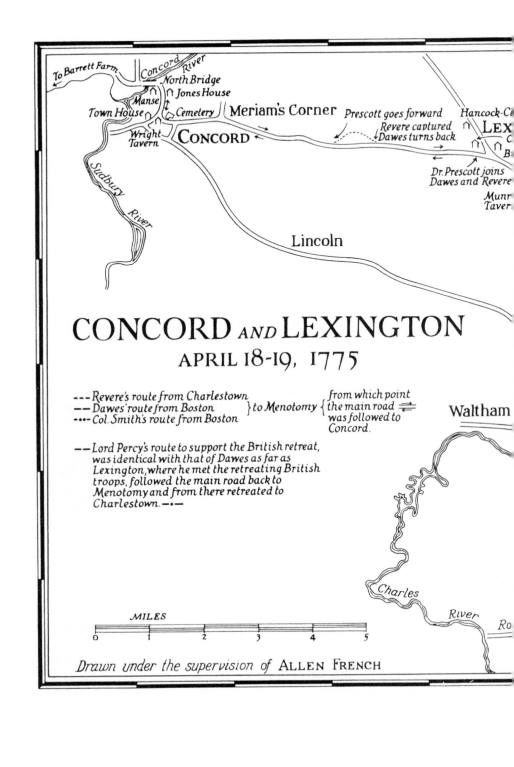

To Barrett Farm
Concord River
North Bridge
Jones House
Manse
Town House
Cemetery
Meriam's Corner
Wright Tavern
CONCORD
Sudbury River

Prescott goes forward
Revere captured
Dawes turns back
Hancock-C
LEX
C
B
Dr. Prescott joins
Dawes and Revere
Munr
Taver

Lincoln

# CONCORD AND LEXINGTON
## APRIL 18-19, 1775

- - - Revere's route from Charlestown.
— — Dawes' route from Boston } to Menotomy {
•••• Col. Smith's route from Boston

from which point
the main road ⇌
was followed to
Concord.

Waltham

— — Lord Percy's route to support the British retreat,
was identical with that of Dawes as far as
Lexington, where he met the retreating British
troops, followed the main road back to
Menotomy and from there retreated to
Charlestown. —•—

Charles
River
Ro

MILES

0       1       2       3       4       5

*Drawn under the supervision of* ALLEN FRENCH

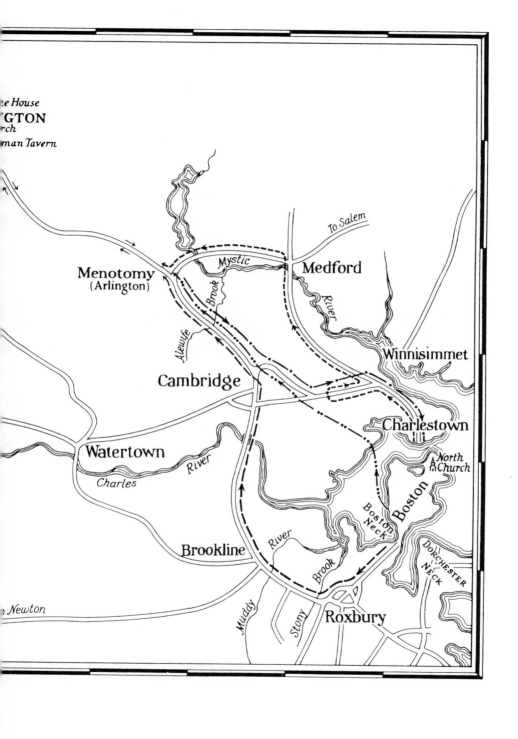

e House
GTON
rch
man Tavern

Menotomy
(Arlington)

To Salem

Mystic

Medford

Brook

River

Alewife

Cambridge

Winnisimmet

Charlestown

Watertown

River

North
Church

Charles

Boston

Brookline

River

Boston
Neck

DORCHESTER
NECK

Brook

Newton

Muddy

Stony

Roxbury

Major Pitcairn's advance guard of light infantry reached Lexington at sunrise. Patches of mist still clung to the grass and shrouded the treetops. It promised to be a lovely spring day.

On Lexington Common, waiting for them, the Redcoats found seventy Minutemen under Captain John Parker, a veteran of the French and Indian War. The Minutemen didn't block the road, but stood quietly on the green with their muskets. Parker didn't want a fight. He planned to stand his ground, firing only if the village was endangered. Pitcairn also wanted to keep the peace, having ordered his troops to hold their fire unless he gave the command personally. There must not be another Boston Massacre.

Pitcairn's troops ran onto the Common and formed a battle line, a long block of men standing three deep. They were in a black mood after a miserable night and not about to take nonsense from Yankees. Muskets poised, the sun glinting off bayonets, they eyed the Minutemen.

*No one today knows who fired the first shot on Lexington Common on April 18, 1775. From a painting by Amos Doolittle.*

Several officers came by on horseback. One waved his sword, shouting: "Ye villains, ye Rebels, disperse! Lay down your arms! Damn you, why don't you lay down your arms?"

Captain Parker, seeing that his men were no match for the regulars, told them to go home. Most had turned to leave when—*bang!* Exactly who fired, Yankee or Redcoat, and why, is a mystery to this day. But the result is well known.

The Redcoats' discipline snapped, as if that one shot had released all their pent-up anger at the colonists. There was an earsplitting crash as hundreds of men fired without orders. The Minutemen replied with a ragged fire that gave one soldier a flesh wound and grazed Pitcairn's horse. When the smoke cleared, eight Americans lay dead on the grass, most shot in the back; nine others were wounded.

Pitcairn let loose a storm of curses. His men had disobeyed an order and he was furious. He drove his horse among them, beating men with the flat of his sword and shouting for them to cease fire. *Cease fire!* Control was restored moments later when Colonel Smith arrived with the main body and the drummers sounded the "Fall-in." The troops cheered and fired a victory salute as they marched out of town. Little did they know how dearly they'd pay for the blood shed on Lexington Common.

The column swept into Concord behind waving flags and musicians playing snappy marching tunes. The commanders and most of their men then broke ranks for breakfast. Invading the village taverns, they demanded food and drink, for which they paid. Chairs were put under the blossoming trees for the officers' comfort.

Search parties, meantime, went to find the patriots' war materials. They knew where to go, because Gage's spies had drawn accurate maps. Yet, to their surprise, they found little of value. Some barrels of flour wound up in a creek. A few

*The shot heard round the world. When Redcoats tried to cross North Bridge outside Concord, they were met with a burst of gunfire from Minutemen assembled on a nearby hill.*

muskets were burned, along with several wooden gun carriages.

Trouble really began when a British patrol tried to secure North Bridge over the Concord River outside the village. Across the way, on a hill overlooking the bridge, hundreds of Minutemen waited. Although outnumbered, the Redcoats prepared to fight; they'd whipped Yankee "rabble" in Lexington and felt confident.

The Minutemen would probably have stayed on their hill had they not seen the smoke of the burning gun carriages rising from Concord. "They're burning the town," someone cried, and they moved forward. The Redcoats fired warning shots, then a volley, killing two. "Fire, fellow soldiers, for God's sake, fire!" shouted Colonel John Buttrick, the American commander. Three Redcoats fell dead, nine wounded, while

their comrades ran off as fast as their legs could carry them. The Minutemen didn't follow, but went home or returned to their hill. The fight at Concord—it could hardly be called a battle—had lasted about three minutes. Yet in that time the farmers had fired "the shot heard round the world."

At noon, after four hours in Concord, Colonel Smith declared his mission accomplished. Bugles sounded. Drums beat. Sergeants bawled commands. Redcoats formed columns and began the return march to Boston. The Americans let them go peacefully until they were a mile from the village. That's when the sky seemed to fall.

Minutemen and militia had been drawn to Concord from miles around in answer to the alarms. Singly and in small groups, nearly four thousand men stationed themselves along the Concord–Lexington Road. Not that you'd have seen more than a handful of them at any given time. But they were there, hidden behind open windows, rail fences, trees, rocks, and stone walls. Firing from cover, they sent a hail of lead into the densely packed columns. Even women lent a hand; a Redcoat told of seeing a woman blazing away from a window with an ancient blunderbuss, a type of shotgun used by the Puritans.

This was something new for the Redcoats, something for which their training hadn't prepared them. European regulars were not taught to think for themselves. They were uniformed machines programmed to advance in closed ranks to within a few yards of the enemy. Then, on command, each side fired its muskets in massed volleys. Nobody aimed, because aiming wasn't taught; muskets were so inaccurate that they didn't even have a rear gunsight. And they were dangerous. Unless the wind came from behind, soldiers turned their heads away just before firing to avoid the flashback when the gunpowder went off, because it might blind them. The idea was for many men to point their guns in the same direction, fire at once, reload quickly, and fire again in the hope of hitting something.

In regular battle, volley after volley was exchanged, creating the "fog of battle," clouds of gunsmoke that made men sneeze and cry. Troops kept firing, ignoring the dead and wounded around them; the moment a man fell, someone in a rear rank took his place. A bullet, a one-ounce lead ball, could maim a person, breaking bones and tearing entire muscles from arms and legs. If one side seemed to be winning, it stopped shooting and charged with bayonets, fourteen inches of cold steel. British regulars were considered the best in the world with the bayonet.

Tough as they were, the Redcoats didn't know how to deal with the Americans. Not that their attackers were especially good shots. Their guns were just as inaccurate as those of the British, and experts estimate that only one out of every three hundred bullets found its mark that day. But that didn't matter, because heavy firing from invisible gunmen terrified the regulars. "What an unfair method of carrying on a war," one complained in a letter home. Americans, he felt, didn't play by the rules of "civilized warfare."

The columns plodded onward, leaving a trail of dead and dying. Nearing Lexington, men panicked, broke ranks, and ran into the village. They were sprawled on the ground, panting, when a band struck up "Yankee Doodle." Lord Percy had come with the reserves. His Lordship had the beaten troops move on while hundreds of his own men acted as flankers. These troops fanned out on either side of the road to flush snipers from hiding. They were merciless. Anyone caught with a weapon died on the spot.

Flankers, breaking into houses, terrorized people and stole whatever they could carry. Anything had value to these poorly paid men: candle stubs, pen nibs, pewter cups. One soldier took a Latin grammar, although he probably didn't know a word of that language. But it was a book and had some resale value.

The retreat continued until sunset, when the columns stumbled across Charlestown Neck to safety on Bunker Hill. The Yankees didn't follow them, for fear of being shot at from the hill and by warships cruising offshore. So ended the Nineteenth of April of 'Seventy-five, a day full of history. The Redcoats had lost 73 killed, 174 wounded, and 26 missing. American losses were 49 dead and 42 wounded and missing.

Everyone knew the meaning of the skirmishes that day, even the boys at Boston's Latin School. The headmaster dismissed them sadly: "War's begun—school's done."

NEWS OF LEXINGTON and Concord swept New England. Within days, ten thousand men were camped outside Boston, daring Gage to come out and fight. But the general wasn't going anywhere—yet. He had a strong position in Boston. Command of the sea guaranteed supplies from home. Reinforcements, he knew, had already sailed and would arrive late in May. Until then, there was nothing to do but sit tight and hope for the best.

Meantime, bad news kept coming. On May 10, 1775, the king's forces lost Fort Ticonderoga, one of the most important strongholds in North America. Built on a hill on the New York side of Lake Champlain, "Ti" controlled water traffic between Canada and the Hudson River Valley. Whoever held Ti could stab into Canada from the south or, coming down from the north, cut off New England from the rest of the colonies. The rebels had had to take it.

Although Fort Ticonderoga had become rundown after the French and Indian War, its fifty-odd Redcoats could easily have chopped an invading force to pieces with their cannon. The rebels sent against Ti, however, weren't about to throw themselves in front of cannon. These were the Green Mountain Boys, who took their name from the mountains of their native Vermont. The area, then a wilderness claimed by New York and New Hampshire, lay opposite Ti on the eastern shore of Lake Champlain. Vermont became our fourteenth state in 1792.

The Green Mountain Boys were led by Ethan Allen, at thirty-six a living legend. Tall and fair-haired, he was said to be strong as an ox and brave as a lion. Settlers spent wintry nights telling about how he bit off the heads of nails and strangled bears with his bare hands. Allen once fought two men, they said. Actually, it wasn't a fight, because he grabbed one in each hand, lifted them off the ground, and banged them together until they begged for mercy.

Allen was joined by a dark, sour little man in the uniform of the Connecticut militia. His name was Benedict Arnold and he seemed to spit acid with every word. Most people disliked him at first sight. Yet this thirty-four-year-old druggist was a born soldier, one of the best America ever produced.

In the early hours of May 10, an eighty-five-man assault force rowed across Lake Champlain from the Vermont shore. Clouds drifted across the face of the moon, casting patches of light and shadow on the calm lake. The rowers dipped their oars rhythmically, quietly, until the boats grounded a few hundred yards south of the fort. Nothing stirred, save the night creatures scurrying in the underbrush.

The Green Mountain Boys crept up to the fort, hoping to find a way in without being seen. Luckily for them, a small side entrance stood open next to the gate. Two sentries, one outside, one inside, stood guard. Everyone else slept.

The outside guard saw the raiders' approach and, pointing his musket straight at Allen's chest, pulled the trigger. *Pfft!* The gunpowder fizzled and flashed, but didn't explode. Amazed, the sentry dropped his musket and ran inside, shouting at the top of his voice. His companion stepped out and lunged at Allen with his bayonet. The big fellow sidestepped and whacked him over the head with the flat of his sword, sending him to his knees.

Whooping and hollering, the Green Mountain Boys burst into the fort. In front of them was a parade ground with barracks to the left and across the way. Immediately they formed ranks and leveled their muskets at the darkened windows.

Allen bounded up a flight of stairs to the officers' quarters, shouting for the fort's commander: "Come out of there, you damned old rat!" But instead of the commander, he

*"In the name of the Great Jehovah and the Continental Congress."*
*Ethan Allen announces the capture of Fort Ticonderoga to its surprised*
*commander.*

met Lieutenant Jocelyn Feltham. The young man, half-naked, had the presence of mind to ask in whose name he invaded His Majesty's property. Allen's voice boomed: "In the name of the Great Jehovah and the Continental Congress." The fort's commander, Captain William Delaplace, came out of his room a moment later. Allen shouted that he'd better surrender or the garrison would be massacred. Delaplace surrendered.

Ti had cost Great Britain many lives and months of fighting during the French and Indian War. Ethan Allen took it in ten minutes without firing a shot and with no damage, save a sentry's sore head.

GAGE HAD better news two weeks later, when sails appeared on the horizon. Next morning, May 25, 1775, transports anchored in Boston Harbor. His reinforcements had arrived.

The ships carried 2,500 men, the flower of the British army. Leading them were three major generals—Sir William Howe, Sir Henry Clinton, and John Burgoyne—said to be the best battlefield officers in the service. Sir William Howe, the senior man, was a cousin of the king. Although a heavy drinker and a reckless gambler, he was also a war hero, having guided General Wolfe's army up the Quebec cliffs to the Plains of Abraham in 1759. Sir Henry Clinton, a professional soldier since becoming a lieutenant at thirteen, was a veteran of campaigns against the French in Europe. Quick-tempered and snobbish, he trusted no one and suspected everyone of wanting to ruin his career. Troops called John Burgoyne "Gentleman Johnny," not because of his manners, but because he was a gentle man. The common soldier, Burgoyne believed, should be treated as a human being, not whipped as an animal. He even insisted that officers not swear at their men.

While nearing the coast, the three generals were on the bridge of their flagship as it passed a New England vessel. A lieutenant "spoke" the vessel, calling to its captain for the latest news. The generals were shocked to learn that their comrades were besieged in Boston. "What!" thundered Gentleman Johnny. "Ten thousand peasants keep five thousand king's troops shut up? Well, let *us* get in, and we'll soon find elbowroom!" Redcoats cheered, and from then on Burgoyne had another nickname: General Elbow Room. He'd soon hate its very sound.

Burgoyne's remark was meant as a little joke. But, it gives us a glimpse of the attitude of Britain's war leaders. These men committed the soldier's worst sin: They held their enemy in contempt. They thought of Americans as fools, yokels, play-soldiers, Yankee Doodles—no match for His Majesty's regulars. Lexington and Concord held no lessons, carried no warnings, for them. The rebels, they told themselves, had been lucky and had fought dirty. Next time would be different, they vowed. They were right, only they didn't know how different until it was too late.

General Gage saw a chance to kill two birds with one stone. He'd noticed that the Dorchester Peninsula controlled Boston's southern approaches. By ferrying part of his seventy-five-hundred-man army across the harbor, he could break the siege and seize Cambridge, where the Massachusetts militia had their main camp on the grounds of Harvard College.

Plans were carefully made but, as usual, secrets couldn't be kept in Boston. Gentleman Johnny boasted of the plan and soon General Artemas Ward, commander of the militia, knew its details. Ward decided to strike first. On June 16, 1775, he ordered twelve hundred militiamen to cross Charlestown Neck. Mission: build a fort on Bunker Hill. This 110-foot, round-topped hill commanded Boston from the north. Cannon placed there could blast the town and the docks, forcing Gage to withdraw.

That night the militiamen filed past Mark's cage and halted at the foot of Bunker Hill. Their commander was forty-three-year-old Colonel William Prescott of Pepperell, Massachusetts. A tall, lean man, Prescott had served brilliantly in the French and Indian War. The British admired his skill and offered to make him a colonel in the regular army, a rare honor for a colonial. He refused, preferring instead to be a farmer in his home colony.

Next to Prescott stood fifty-three-year-old Israel Putnam. "Old Put," as everyone called him, was a human firecracker, hot-tempered, loud, and bursting with energy. Also a hero of the French and Indian War, he still had many friends in the British army. Although a general of the Connecticut militia, in Massachusetts he was only a volunteer with no authority over Prescott. Yet that didn't prevent him from offering advice, which was listened to with respect.

Tonight Old Put gave terrible advice. He said it would be a mistake to dig in on Bunker Hill, because the militia's light cannon couldn't reach the ships in the harbor from there. Just south of Bunker Hill, and connected to it by a low ridge, was Breed's Hill. Although only seventy-five feet high, it was closer to targets in Boston. Its western slope leveled out near Charlestown, deserted since April for fear of British raids. Snipers hidden in the houses could pick off Redcoats advancing up the hill, Putnam insisted.

Prescott listened, argued that he had his orders, and finally agreed to fortify Breed's Hill. Although the Revolution's most famous battle was fought there, for some unknown reason colonists called it the Battle of Bunker Hill. History books borrowed the name, and that's what we'll call it.

Prescott began work on a redoubt, an earthen fort 160 feet long by 80 feet wide with walls 6 feet high and a foot thick. Digging was farmers' work, and his men were experts with pick and shovel. It was a clear, warm night, and they could hear the clocks of Boston strike midnight. Down below, bobbing gently in the Charles and Mystic rivers, were HMS *Lively, Symmetry, Falcon,* and *Glasgow,* mounting between them seventy-five heavy cannon. The sixty-eight-gun *Somerset* rode at anchor near Long Wharf. "Dig, men, dig," Prescott cried. "Dig for your lives!" They had to be under cover by sunrise or be exposed to those iron-throated monsters.

Prescott realized at first light that he shouldn't have taken Putnam's advice. His men were in a sack and the enemy held the drawstring. Breed's Hill was vulnerable on both its Charlestown and Mystic River sides. With no fort on Bunker Hill, the enemy could sweep around the redoubt. The British could occupy Charlestown Neck and wait for the rebels to surrender or starve. Or they could attack the redoubt from behind, turning it into a slaughter pen.

Prescott had no choice but to do the best with what he had. Militiamen were sent to take up sniping positions in the abandoned town. Hundreds of others were sent to build a breastwork jutting from the redoubt toward the Mystic River. A breastwork is a trench with earth piled in front.

The breastwork was taking shape when boatswain whistles brought the warships to life. Bare feet slapped on planking as gun crews raced to battle stations. Slowly helmsmen swung their vessels broadside to the shore.

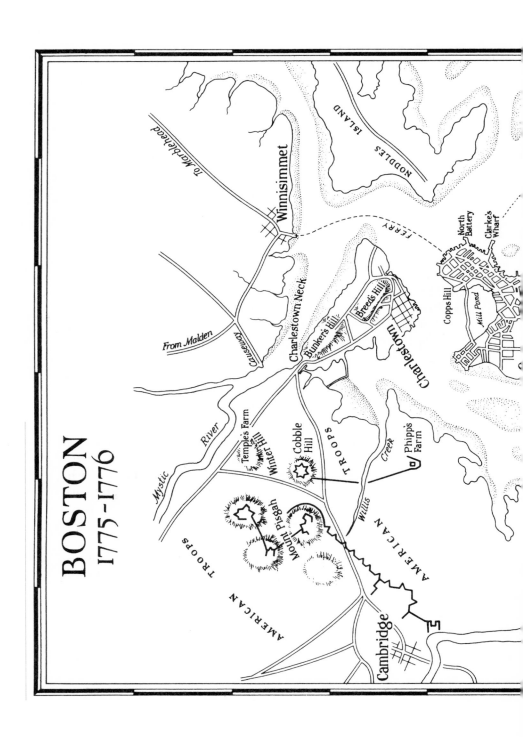

## BOSTON
### 1775–1776

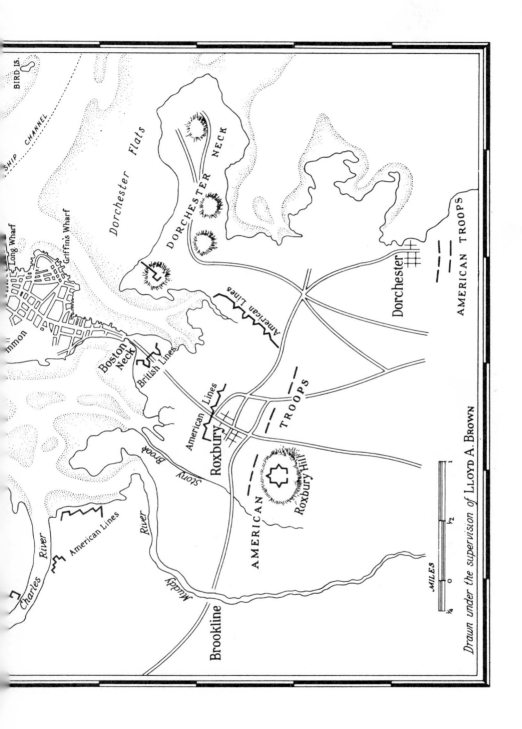

BIRD IS.

SHIP CHANNEL

Dorchester Flats

DORCHESTER NECK

Long Wharf

Griffin's Wharf

mmon

Boston Neck

British Lines

American Lines

Dorchester

AMERICAN TROOPS

American Lines

Roxbury

American Lines

TROOPS

AMERICAN

Roxbury Hill

Stony Brook

Charles River

American Lines

Muddy

River

Brookline

MILES

⅛  0  ½

*Drawn under the supervision of* LLOYD A. BROWN

Bostonians were jolted awake by thundering naval guns. Rushing to their windows, they saw the ships rock as the guns went into action. Clouds of gray smoke were already rolling across the harbor when an ear-splitting roar came from the town itself: The big guns of the Copp's Hill Battery had joined the bombardment.

Nearly two hundred British cannon banged away with solid shot, iron balls weighing as much as twenty-four pounds each. Balls came over with a loud whoosh before they tore into the hillside, plowing long, straight furrows. Some hit the redoubt with a sharp whack, burying themselves in its walls. The militiamen, few of whom had ever heard a cannon fired, let alone fired at them, hugged the ground, trembling.

Suddenly some diggers gasped in horror. Asa Pollard, a big, happy farm boy, hadn't ducked quickly enough. Friends saw him take a few steps before collapsing. But he was no longer the Asa they knew. His head was gone, his neck a fountain of gushing blood.

Prescott saw his men go pale. Quickly, before panic gripped them and they fled, he leaped onto the wall, deliberately exposing himself. "It was a one-in-a-million shot," he cried. Iron balls whooshed harmlessly overhead, or plowed the hillside, without coming near him. Although most men returned to work, many had seen enough. Now and throughout the day, hundreds deserted. Among them were the crews of the redoubt's four cannon, who pulled out after firing only a few shots. Cowardice as well as courage was plentiful at the Battle of Bunker Hill.

Meanwhile, the British generals watched the scene. Abijah Willard, a Bostonian loyal to the king, stood at Gage's side as he studied the redoubt through a spyglass. After a while, Gage handed Willard the spyglass, asking if he knew the tall fellow on the wall. He did. It was his brother-in-law, William Prescott.

"Will he fight?" Gage asked.

Willard's reply stunned him: "I cannot answer for his men, but Prescott will fight you to the gates of hell."

The generals' plan called for Sir William Howe to deliver a right hook followed by a left jab. Howe would send his light infantry along the unguarded beach of the Mystic River and sweep around the American rear. At the same time, grenadiers and regular units would attack along a broad front near Charlestown. This plan promised not only to avenge Lexington and Concord, but beat the rebels so badly that they'd lose faith in their cause.

At 1:30 P.M., June 17, 1775, a double line of barges cast off from Long Wharf. Their passengers sat at attention, bolt upright, eyes straight ahead, not moving a muscle or saying a word. Muskets and bayonets, badges and buttons, winked and flashed in the sun. Slowly, ever so slowly, the oarsmen pulled for the Charlestown shore.

The rebels on Breed's Hill were too busy strengthening their positions to notice this gorgeous pageant. Prescott ordered Captain Thomas Knowlton's two hundred Connecticut militiamen to extend the breastwork to the bank of the Mystic. Luckily, they found a low stone fence with two upper rails of wood. Knowlton's men tore rails from nearby fences and jammed them between the two rails, together with stones and clumps of grass to conceal themselves from the enemy.

The defenses were nearly completed when Captain John Stark arrived from Cambridge with eight hundred New Hampshire militia. Stark, a veteran of scores of Indian fights, distributed his men along the rail fence. He also ruined Howe's plan for a right hook. At the edge of the riverbank, where the fence ended, he noticed a gap between the bank and the water. At low tide the gap was twelve feet wide, enough for the British to pass around the rebel flank. Stark had his men roll rocks down the riverbank to form a low stone wall.

When Howe came ashore, he found the rebel defenses stronger than they'd been in the morning. As his men settled down to lunch, he sent to Boston for another regiment of infantry and for Major Pitcairn's First Battalion of Marines, bringing his strength to twenty-five hundred.

Howe divided his troops into three strike forces. The light infantry mustered on the beach opposite the stone wall. Howe joined the grenadiers in the center, facing the rail fence and breastwork. Regular infantry and marines under General Robert Pigot waited on the left, near Charlestown.

The Redcoats stood in the open, one rank behind the other, their battleflags unfurled. Howe walked along the silent ranks, proud as any general could be. "Gentlemen," he said, ignoring the bombardment booming overhead, "I am very happy in having the honor of commanding so fine a body of men. I do not in the least doubt that you will behave like Englishmen and as becomes good soldiers. . . . I shall not desire any one of you to go a step further than where I go myself at your head." He'd lead the grenadiers personally, a perfect target in scarlet, white, and gold.

The troops were awaiting his signal to advance when snipers opened fire from Charlestown. Pigot's men began to fall. Howe delayed the assault only long enough to order the town burned. On the ships' gundecks, sailors drew "hot shot," cannonballs heated red-hot, out of ovens with tongs. Gunners in the Copp's Hill Battery loaded "carcasses," hollow balls filled with sulphur and pitch.

Charlestown became an inferno. Within minutes, every building was sending clouds of sparks skyward. Most of the snipers fled, but a few fearless fellows dashed from one hide-out to another, dropping Redcoats even as flames crackled around them.

Spectators crowded the rooftops of Boston, scarcely believing their eyes. War was more terrible than they'd imagined in their worst nightmares. At Braintree, ten miles to the southeast, people watched from the summit of Penn's Hill. Abigail Adams held the hand of the seven-year-old who'd grow up to be the sixth president of the United States.

At Howe's signal, drummers began a long roll. The Redcoats, sweltering in their woolen uniforms, the straps of their packs cutting into their shoulders, stepped out to the attack. They moved under a forest of glinting bayonets, as if on

*Sir William Howe led the charge up Bunker Hill and later commanded British forces in America.*

parade. They moved in silence, except for the scraping of boots and the tapping of the drums, which set the marching pace. The bombardment stopped so as not to hit them by accident.

The Americans stared wide-eyed. Behind those bayonets were British regulars, the finest troops on earth. And they were coming for *them!*

The drums grew louder.

Mouths dry, stomachs knotted with fear, the Americans waited, nervously fingering their triggers. One panicky farm boy could have caused the whole line to fire with the enemy still out of range.

Old Put rode behind the rail fence. "Don't fire until you see the whites of their eyes," he cried, "then fire low." The whites of their eyes—good advice, since there was little chance of killing anyone with a musket beyond forty yards. Firing low meant that the musket's recoil, which threw the weapon up, would send bullets into the enemy's belly and chest. For good measure, many rebel guns were loaded with "buck and ball," four pieces of buckshot with each bullet to increase killing power.

Howe's light infantry moved down the beach with steady, measured steps. Their orders were to take the stone wall without firing a shot. Today they'd use only the bayonet.

Closer, closer they came until their faces were clearly visible under their hats. Down went the bayonets into the charge position. *"Huzzah!"* they shouted and ran forward.

Suddenly there was the clatter of metal on stone and the wall bristled with muskets.

Now!

The wall seemed to explode in the faces of the light infantry. A sheet of orange flame lashed out, followed by the thud of lead striking flesh. Soldiers were spun around by the bullets' force, crumpling to the sand or falling into the water.

Still the Redcoats wouldn't give up. Again and again officers beat them into ranks with the flat of the sword and sent them forward. Each time they met a blast of musketry. Each time the survivors retreated, leaving their dead two deep in places. Finally they turned and fled down the beach, away from that wall of death.

Howe did no better. His grenadiers were almost to the rail fence when the Americans fired. It was as if they'd been mowed down by a gigantic scythe. Bodies lay in rows, keeping ranks even in death. Although most of his aides went down around him, Howe walked away without a scratch.

Rebels cheered and whistled after the fleeing Redcoats. Prescott and other experienced officers, however, knew that the fight had only begun. They also knew that it would be harder next time, since fewer than nine hundred defenders remained. Men deserted in droves either from cowardice or because they felt they'd had enough fighting for one day. As many as six men were seen "helping" someone with a slight flesh wound to the rear.

Losing the first round hardened Howe's determination to win. Within fifteen minutes, the drums announced another attack. Light infantry and grenadiers marched together toward the rail fence. On the British left, Pigot's men went for the redoubt and breastwork. There would be no more attacks on the beach wall.

Once again Howe led the way. The ranks advanced behind him as one man, stepping over mangled bodies and broken equipment from the first attack. Now and then they heard moans or saw a wounded man lift an arm to show that he was still alive. They kept moving, neither pausing nor looking down. There'd be time enough for the wounded later.

When they were twenty yards from the rail fence, Old Put gave the order: "Fire!"

The meadow became a scene from hell. Redcoats lay in the high grass, some dead, others thrashing and screaming in pain. Ralph Farnum of New Hampshire carried their screams in his memory for life. In 1855, Farnum was 105 years old and the last survivor of Bunker Hill. The screaming, he said, "was louder than the firearms" and made him too sick to fire his gun again.

Among those who kept firing were black Minutemen. Free blacks, either escaped slaves or those freed by their

owners, were common in eighteenth-century New England.
At least twelve blacks fought at Bunker Hill. Peter Salem,
whose master freed him so he could enlist, first saw action
at Concord. Cuff Whittemore, Caesar Bason, and Barzillai
Lew stood behind the breastwork and rail fence. Salem Poor's
courage was noted in an official report, which said he "be-
haved like an experienced officer as well as an excellent soldier."

Friendship proved stronger than the hatreds of war even
at Bunker Hill. Rebels were firing at an officer when Old
Put caught a glimpse of his face. It was a friend, Major John
Small. "For God's sake, spare that man," Putnam shouted,
"I love him as a brother." Small, recognizing the voice, bowed
to his friend for saving his life, then turned and walked out
of range.

Howe, who'd come through again without a scratch, noticed that his white breeches were streaked with blood from
the grass. "There was a moment I never felt before," he'd
say later. He'd often led men in battle, and he was used to
death. But he'd never seen men slaughtered so easily and
in such numbers. Yet he didn't give up. Without hesitating,
he sent for Sir Henry Clinton and the reserves from Boston.
But his force was so battered that, if he failed again, he
knew he'd have to admit defeat. That frightened him more
than death itself.

American losses so far were thirty killed and wounded,
compared to hundreds for the enemy. But as they checked
their ammunition, Prescott's men knew that the end was near.
Most had only two or three shots left. If these couldn't halt
the next charge, they'd be up against bayonets, a weapon
they neither had nor were trained to use.

A hush fell over the battlefield as Howe's artillery ceased
fire.

The drums set the pace as the Redcoats stepped out
again. This time Howe had them remove their knapsacks;
most also took off their coats to fight in shirtsleeves.

The drumbeats quickened. The scarlet ranks swept forward, over the dead, over the wounded, over the grass slippery with blood.

A volley crashed into them. Redcoats fell. Others stepped into their places. Now they were angry. "Push on! Push on!" men shouted to one another. "Conquer or die!"

Major Pitcairn led his marines right into the flaming gun muzzles. Suddenly Peter Salem fired a shot from the redoubt. Down went Pitcairn. His son, a marine lieutenant, rushed to his side. His father ordered him back to his men, but he refused and helped carry his father off the battlefield. The major was dying.

Nobody can say how far the Redcoats could have gone if the rebels hadn't run out of ammunition. Firing sputtered out and the Redcoats swarmed over the wall of the redoubt. The battle became a brawl with men trying to kill each other any way they could. Yelling and cursing, the Redcoats lunged and slashed with bayonets. Rebels fought with clubbed muskets, knives, rocks, fists, teeth. Gradually they fought their way out of the redoubt. At the same time, the men at the breastwork and rail fence backed off, firing their last shots to cover their comrades' escape. There was no panic, but an orderly withdrawal to Cambridge. Prescott refused even to run, but walked to the rear proudly, showing the enemy his back.

Sir William Howe had his hill but little else. There was no joy in victory or satisfaction at a job well done, for his army was too badly mauled to go after the fleeing rebels. American losses numbered 138 killed and 276 wounded, suffered mostly in the storming of the redoubt. Among the dead was Doctor Joseph Warren. British losses were horrifying: 226 killed and 828 wounded, or 46 to 48 percent of

OVERLEAF:
*The death of Dr. Joseph Warren as the British storm the redoubt on Bunker Hill. John Trumbull, who painted this picture, knew many of the participants in the battle. The black man on the extreme right is Peter Salem, who shot Major Pitcairn.*

the attacking force. No army in our age of automatic weapons and high explosives has taken such punishment in less than three hours.

All was confusion in Boston as the Redcoats brought back their dead and wounded. Throughout the night and well into the next day, people stared at war's human wreckage. Soldiers' wives crowded the waterfront, anxiously looking for the one face they hoped to see. The lucky ones fell in behind their men as they stepped ashore. Often the news was bad, filling the air with widows' wails.

Boston's hospitals resembled butcher shops with bleeding, moaning men lying thick on the floors outside the surgeons' rooms. Major Pitcairn's son staggered about, dazed from a wound. "I have lost my father," he told a brother officer, tears streaming down his cheeks. Nearby a wounded marine sergeant of twenty years' service whispered gently, "We have all lost a father." But at least the major was out of his misery. The sufferings of the wounded had just begun.

Being treated for gunshot wounds tested one's courage as nothing else could. There were no painkillers. The patient was given a bottle of whiskey, if whiskey was available. When the liquor took effect and his head spun, the surgeon's helpers made him "bite the bullet"—put a bullet between his teeth to prevent him from biting off his tongue during the operation. Then they held him down while the surgeon went to work.

In a simple operation, the surgeon searched for the bullet with a finger or an iron probe, removing it with extractors, long forceps with a tiny cup at each end. Head wounds called for trepanning, boring into the skull with a tool like a corkscrew to relieve pressure on the brain. Surgeons deserved the nickname "sawbones," for amputation was the favorite treatment of wounds to the limbs. Any saw would do, even one from a carpenter's toolbox. Young surgeons were advised by their elders to ignore their patients' screams and saw away as quickly as possible. The stump was then cauterized, seared with a red-hot blade to stop bleeding. Such treatments caused

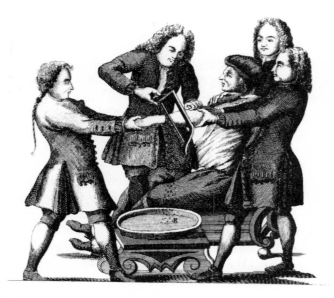

*This drawing from an eighteenth-century book shows a standard treatment for gunshot. Although the man in the picture seems to be taking the treatment calmly, we know that many patients died of shock, pain, and loss of blood.*

many to die of pain, shock, and loss of blood. Deep wounds to the stomach or chest couldn't be treated at all; victims were often left to die on the battlefield rather than have them occupy scarce hospital space.

There were no antibiotics, and no knowledge that dirt causes infection. Wounds weren't washed, and surgeons cleaned their hands after operating, not before. If an instrument fell on the ground, the surgeon picked it up and kept cutting. The same scalpel, uncleaned, was used on scores of patients. Bandages might be anything from a bedsheet cut into strips to an old flag.

American hospitals were no better than the enemy's. Benjamin Rush, a famous doctor, called them "Sinks of Human Life in the army . . . [that] robbed the United States of more citizens than the sword." We know from soldiers' diaries that many feared their own army surgeons more than enemy soldiers.

THE BATTLE OF BUNKER HILL was a turning point for both sides. It gave the Americans encouragement, proving that they could whip European professionals. It taught the British some lessons in humility. Nobody laughed at Gentleman Johnny's joke anymore. "We have got a little elbow-room," an officer said, "but I think we have paid too dearly for it."

Back in England, Bunker Hill encouraged people to speak out against the war. The government, they said, was forcing Americans into rebellion, and that was wrong. Army officers resigned rather than fight the colonists, among them Lord Effingham, whose ancestor had led the fleet of Queen Elizabeth I against the Spanish Armada. "The people at large love the Americans," wrote a visitor to London. Yet none of this mattered to George III, who had his friends in Parliament vote to treat the Americans as a foreign enemy. There was nothing to discuss, as far as His Majesty was concerned.

It was going to be a long, hard struggle.

MEANTIME, in Philadelphia, the Second Continental Congress voted to create an American army, June 14, 1775. Actually, it created two types of armed forces. The Continental or regular army was formed by units sent by the colonies; Congress began by adopting Artemas Ward's army outside Boston. Each soldier, called a Continental, enlisted for a fixed term or for the entire war, earning $6.66 a month. In addition, each colony had its own militia for use at home or to lend to the Continental Army as needed.

John Adams wanted the quiet man in the militia colonel's uniform to lead the army. George Washington, he knew, was a respected patriot and, better yet, a Southerner. With him in command, the Southern colonies would surely join New England in the war. Thus, on June 15, Adams nominated and Congress voted in the Virginian as commander in chief of the "Grand American Army."

Washington wasn't happy with his post. He took the speaker's platform and, looking out at the audience, said firmly: "I do not think myself equal to the Command I am honored with."

Lord knows he had reason to be unhappy. He knew that the command would be more like a thornbush than a bed of roses. He'd never led an army or won a battle. His only experience was in leading frontier militia during the French and Indian War. Given a choice, he'd rather have led a regiment, even shouldered a musket as a private, he wrote in private letters. But since Congress wanted him, he pushed aside his doubts and resolved to do his best.

George Washington came to embody the American Revolution, and for that reason we must know him better. He stood six feet tall and weighed over two hundred pounds. Broad-shouldered, he had long arms and legs, and enormous hands. Yet, despite his size, he moved gracefully. A natural in the saddle, he was said to be the finest horseman in America.

Washington wasn't handsome. He had a large red nose, gray-blue eyes, and a face pitted with smallpox scars. His voice was sometimes difficult to understand because of his teeth, which were false. Although otherwise healthy, poor teeth made him miserable all his adult life. He had countless pairs of dentures made from wood, hippopotamus ivory, and the teeth of humans, cows, pigs, and elk. One pair of false teeth was set in lead, weighed three pounds, and was connected with heavy steel springs. No wonder he seldom smiled.

Grave and serious, Washington seemed to have an invisible wall between himself and others. No one—except perhaps his darling wife Patsy—ever got close to him or shared his innermost thoughts and feelings. No one told jokes about him or gave him a nickname. We know of only one man who dared use his first name, and that he did on a bet. "Good morning, George!" said his friend Gouverneur Morris, clapping him on the back. Washington said nothing, but his icy glance told Morris that he'd gone too far.

Washington's real strengths were not physical but moral. Thomas Jefferson, who knew him well, described him as "a wise, a good, and a great man." Truer words were never spoken. Although the story that he was unable to lie about cutting down his father's prize cherry tree is a myth, it comes close to the heart of the man. He had a keen sense of responsibility and devotion to duty. Congress had given him a job to do, and he'd do it honestly. He took no pay, since he wanted to make no profit from patriotism; all he asked was that Congress repay him the money he laid out of his own pocket. At the end of the war, auditors found an error of less than one dollar in his accounts.

No man cared more for the soldiers' welfare than the commander in chief. He wrote thousands of letters badgering Congress to pay them or send them vital supplies, such as food and blankets. Common soldiers called him "Excellency" and "The General" out of deepest respect. But they also knew that he respected them, that he held their lives precious and would never waste them in foolish schemes. On dark nights, when the wind howled and rain fell in sheets, he'd find time to talk with a homesick youngster on guard duty.

In 1754, when he was twenty-two, Washington had his first taste of war. "I heard the bullets whistle, and believe me," he said, "there is something charming in the sound." But his boyish enthusiasm quickly passed as he learned about war the hard way. War was not charming, only nasty and ugly. This realization made him the greatest of America's citizen-soldiers. Unlike professionals, who make war a career, he hated it. War, he knew, was sometimes necessary, but it was an evil nevertheless. He was the one irreplaceable man, and without him America almost certainly couldn't have won its Revolution.

THE COMMANDER IN CHIEF found an army of fifteen thousand waiting for him when he took over from Artemas Ward at Cambridge, July 2, 1775. Volunteers marched in each day, sometimes from as far away as Maryland and Virginia. These Southerners were called "shirtmen" after their buckskin hunting shirts, which came down to the knees and were tied at the waist with a leather belt. Shirtmen came from the frontier and were as cunning and fierce as their Indian enemies.

The shirtman's favorite weapon was the long rifle. A *rifle* had an extra-long barrel into which spiral grooves, or "riflings," were cut to make the bullet spin in flight. Slower to load than the musket, it made up for this disadvantage with greater range and accuracy. A sharpshooter could easily hit a target at three hundred yards; an exceptionally good shot might pick off a man a half-mile away. Shirtmen were fond of their rifles, giving them pet names such as Betsy and Nancy, Hot Lips and Little Darlin'.

Washington soon found that he had nearly as many problems as he had men. Gunpowder was scarce and he feared there wouldn't be enough if the British attacked again. Benjamin Franklin came forward with a none-too-helpful suggestion. The noted scientist wanted the army to give up guns in favor of bows and arrows, because an archer could fire four arrows in the time it took to fire one bullet. He didn't explain why, if that was so important, Indians threw away their bows and arrows as soon as they got their hands on guns.

Army discipline gave Washington sleepless nights. Since they were fighting for liberty, many soldiers believed they could do as they pleased. Men refused to salute officers, threatened them, or actually beat them up. Guards left their posts. Soldiers gambled, got drunk, and wrestled in the mud. Their swearing made the general wince.

Washington cracked down within days of his arrival. Each offense was listed, along with its penalty. Failure to salute and swearing carried fines. Fighting brought time in the guardhouse on bread and water. Thieves received thirty-nine lashes on the bare back, later raised to one hundred, but still nothing compared to what a Redcoat received for the same offense.

Washington's efforts paid off—mostly. Yet there were holdouts, like the thirty shirtmen who broke open the guardhouse to free a favorite sergeant. It took five hundred loyal troops to bring them under control.

The general was relieved when a thousand of his men were sent by Congress to capture Quebec to head off a British invasion from Canada. After dreadful hardships in the Maine woods, including near-starvation that drove men to eat dogs and candles, the expedition gathered on the old battlefield of the Plains of Abraham. But they'd come for nothing. General Richard Montgomery, their commander, died in a night battle fought in a blizzard. Benedict Arnold, his aide, took a bullet under the left knee, which lamed him for life. He lay on his cot with two pistols, gritting his teeth, firing off orders, and daring the Redcoats to come after him. Arnold held on through the winter, until the spring thaw and British reinforcements forced a retreat. His courage made him a national hero and won his promotion to brigadier general.

It was also unpleasant outside Boston. As the New England winter closed in, Washington's troops shivered in their huts and counted the days left of their enlistments, most of which expired on New Year's Day, 1776. Fewer than half reenlisted, and the army would have been ruined had Massachusetts and New Hampshire not sent militia units to fill the ranks.

Washington's worst problem, however, was Boston itself. Howe, Gage's replacement as head of British forces in America, had turned Boston into a fortress. There was no way of storming the town or starving out its garrison while the Royal Navy kept the harbor open.

Washington saw that the key to Boston was the high ground of the Dorchester Peninsula. As with Bunker Hill, cannon placed on Dorchester Heights could bombard the town, forcing the British to withdraw or face destruction. Unfortunately, he had only a few cannon, all of which were too small to reach the town. Or so he thought until reminded about Fort Ticonderoga. Ti was a storehouse of big cannon and mortars, short-barreled guns able to throw shells at steep angles.

*Henry Knox was a self-taught soldier, studying gunnery and tactics in his Boston book store.*

Twenty-five-year-old Henry Knox had the job of bringing the guns from Ti. Knox, a jolly three-hundred-pound bookseller, had taught himself gunnery and engineering from books stocked in his Boston shop. He learned well, becoming in time the Continental Army's chief artillery officer.

Knox selected forty-nine pieces of artillery to be moved three hundred miles across snowfields, rivers, and mountains in the dead of winter. He had the guns, each weighing at least one ton, dismounted and tied to heavy sleds pulled by oxen. The guns were then dragged to the Hudson River, floated across on rafts, and hauled over the Berkshires of western Massachusetts. Boston was Washington's for the taking the moment Knox's "nobel train of artillery" skidded into the rebel camp.

At dawn, March 5, 1776—Boston Massacre Day—the British awoke to find cannon looking down on them from Dorchester Heights. Yet Washington held his fire as a signal to Howe that he'd allow him to leave if he didn't burn the town. Howe understood and ordered the evacuation to begin.

On March 17, Boston Harbor seemed filled with a flock of swans about to take flight. The sails of 175 ships were lowered, billowing as they caught the breeze. One by one the vessels filed out of the harbor, bound for Halifax, Nova Scotia, in Canada. With their sailing, not a single Redcoat remained anywhere in the thirteen colonies.

Patriots cheered themselves hoarse. They'd won! They'd beaten the British regulars! The war was over!

Only the tall Virginian kept his peace, unsmiling. He knew the British. They were stubborn, like the bulldogs some regiments kept as mascots. They'd be back.

# · THREE ·

# Times That Tried
# Men's Souls

*A*MERICA owes a great deal to a scruffy Englishman who settled in Philadelphia during the winter of 1774. Thomas Paine was a thin, tight-lipped man with a pickle nose and eyes that seemed to bore through you. Poverty and disappointment had followed him all of his thirty-eight years. Although he'd held many jobs, he'd failed at everything. Failure made him angry at injustice and gave him deep sympathy for the oppressed.

Paine's anger and sympathy remained buried inside him until he arrived in Philadelphia. There he found a job with a small magazine and began to write articles. He wrote about politics, trade, and moral issues like slavery, which he despised. Words—strong, forceful words—flowed easily from his pen.

Paine's talents became important as the American Revolution took shape. By the end of 1775, anyone could see that Great Britain and the colonies were at war. Blood had

*Tom Paine's* **Common Sense** *persuaded countless Americans to demand independence, rather than try to patch up their differences with Great Britain.*

been shed, lives lost, towns burned. Yet most Americans still hoped the quarrel would be patched up and they could continue to be loyal subjects of the British Empire.

Tom Paine did more than anyone to change American minds in favor of independence. In January 1776, he issued *Common Sense*. This forty-two-page pamphlet became the most influential American book ever printed. Aimed at the common people, it called George III "the Royal Brute of Great Britain," a fool who had no right to rule Americans; indeed, Paine believed kings had no right to rule anyone, because all men are equal. Great Britain, he continued, was not the mother country, since mothers don't turn redcoated thugs loose on their children. Americans should not be governed from Europe. No! "Everything that is right or reasonable pleads for separation. The blood of the slain, the weeping voice of nature cries, *'tis time to part.*"

*Common Sense* had the right ideas at the right time and became the first American bestseller. Over 120,000 copies were sold within three months, and still printers couldn't keep up with the demand. Washington wrote from camp outside Boston that his troops were passing *Common Sense* from hand to hand; those who couldn't read sat intently while a comrade read it to them.

Paine lit a fire that leaped across America. Patriots drove out royal governors, took control of colonial assemblies, and held conventions to form new governments. The king's coat of arms came down in one assembly after another and his portraits were turned to the wall. Although independence hadn't been declared, it was quickly becoming a reality.

Some state conventions ordered their delegates at the Second Continental Congress to vote for independence. On June 7, 1776, Richard Henry Lee of Virginia offered a motion to Congress: "RESOLVED, That these United Colonies are, and of right ought to be, free and independent States; that they are absolved from all allegiance to the British Crown; and that all political connection between them and the State of Great Britain is, and ought to be, totally dissolved." But since many delegates weren't ready for such a drastic step as independence, Congress put off voting on the motion for three weeks to allow them to think things over.

*Led by Thomas Jefferson, the drafting committee presents the Declaration of Independence to Congress, July 2, 1776. From a Currier & Ives lithograph.*

Congress, meantime, appointed a five-man committee to draft a declaration of independence. The members of that committee were John Adams (Massachusetts), Benjamin Franklin (Pennsylvania), Roger Sherman (Connecticut), and Robert Livingston (New York). Thomas Jefferson of Virginia, a lanky redhead and at thirty-three the committee's youngest member, was asked to do the actual work because of his "peculiar felicity of expression"; that is, he wrote well.

As Philadelphia baked in summer heat, Jefferson set up a portable desk of his own invention in the parlor of a local bricklayer. He needed no reference books, for he knew

what needed to be said. Within two weeks, by July 2, the draft was ready. After going over it line by line, changing a word here, crossing out a phrase there, Congress adopted Jefferson's Declaration of Independence. Our independence began officially on this date, not July 4, when printed copies of the text were carried by express riders throughout the land.

The Declaration of Independence was read wherever people gathered. Abigail Adams wrote her husband from Boston that, despite the gunpowder shortage, cannon boomed and troops fired volleys in celebration. Crowds in

Worcester, Massachusetts, drank toasts and wished "Perpetual itching and no scratching to America's enemies." Far to the south and west, in the Waxhaws, the unlettered frontiersmen selected a bright nine-year-old as their "public reader." Andy Jackson read the document in his squeaky voice without, he said, getting hoarse or "stopping to spell out the words." And beyond the towering Alleghenies, the men of Boonesborough greeted independence with war whoops.

The parchment copy of the Declaration of Independence familiar to everyone wasn't signed until August 2, 1776. The fifty-five signers knew they were making history. John Hancock, president of the Congress, signed first, writing his name in bold letters so the king could read it without his spectacles.

Others realized they were committing treason and what *that* could mean. Benjamin Harrison of Virginia relieved the tension with humor. Harrison, a fat man, told skinny Elbridge Gerry of Massachusetts that his hanging would be painless: "I shall have the advantage over you on account of my size. All will be over with me in a moment, but you will be kicking in the air half an hour after I am gone."

The Declaration of Independence is really two declarations at once. Jefferson gave most of its space to explaining the colonies' grievances against Great Britain. Most people today neither know nor care about these. The part that concerns us today comes at the beginning. It is this part that has made Jefferson's work a battle cry for oppressed peoples everywhere.

Jefferson began the Declaration of Independence with a ringing defense of liberty: "We hold these truths to be self-evident, that all men are created equal, that they are endowed by their Creator with certain unalienable Rights, that among these are Life, Liberty and the pursuit of Happiness." Governments exist only to protect these rights, which come from God and cannot be given or taken away. When a government fails in its duty, it loses its authority. The people then have the right to abolish it, by force if necessary, and create a new one that will protect their rights.

By "the people," however, Jefferson meant only *free white men*. We must remember that the Founding Fathers belonged to their time, as we belong to ours. And in their time it seemed natural that certain people should rule and that others should be ruled. Women were thought to be weaker and less intelligent than men; they belonged at home with the children, not following careers or participating in government. American women would have to wait until the twentieth century to realize the promise of the Declaration of Independence.

Several signers also owned slaves. Blacks, most believed, were hardly human, so that "liberty" couldn't apply to them. Jefferson himself owned slaves, although he said slavery was wrong and ought to be abolished. "I tremble for my country when I reflect that God is just," he wrote later. Americans had sinned by enslaving blacks and God would punish them, he believed.

Yet Jefferson never freed his slaves, because he felt blacks were inferior and shouldn't mingle with white people. Until they could be returned to Africa, he wanted them kept under kindly masters like himself—as if kindness can substitute for freedom. George Washington, who refused to buy any more slaves, wanted slavery abolished gradually. But that wasn't to be. Slavery was ended suddenly, through a war more terrible than the Revolution.

AMERICANS had declared their independence. Now they would have to fight for it, and not only against the Redcoats. The Declaration of Independence was not welcomed everywhere. Historians estimate that only one-third of the people favored the Revolution. Another third were fence-sitters who wanted to see which side would win before committing themselves. Personal safety and property counted more with them than the ideals of liberty and independence. When the British were winning, they sang "God Save the King." When the Continentals had the upper hand, they boasted of their patriotism. The final third called themselves Loyalists, because they remained loyal to the king and opposed the Revolution. Patriots called them Tories, an Irish slang word for outlaws. A Tory, they said, "is a thing whose head is in England, whose body is in America, and whose neck needs stretching."

Being a Tory was a matter of conscience, not money. No rule said that one type of person should favor the Revolution, another the king. Rich and poor, people of every occupation and walk of life favored each side. Tories, too, believed that taxation without representation was tyranny, but nothing compared to revolution, a crime that violated all law. If the Revolution succeeded, they believed America would become a jungle with people using violence whenever anything displeased them. Gun-law would become the law of the land.

Patriots disagreed. They believed they were fighting for the noblest cause of all: liberty. Fearing enemies behind their backs, they wanted to identify Tories and prevent them from doing harm. Thus, town governments insisted that everyone sign an oath of loyalty to the United States, pledging to defend it against the king. Those whose conscience wouldn't let them sign, or let them lie to protect themselves, were branded enemies of their country.

A witch-hunt began. At first Tories were humiliated in ways that, however silly, caused bitterness. When a young Tory appeared at a quilting bee, girls stripped him to the waist and smeared him with molasses and cattail down in imitation of tar and feathers. Militiamen once grabbed a Tory, took his pants, and made him sit on ice "to cool his loyalty."

Things turned really nasty as the war continued and the patriots suffered defeats. Tory shopkeepers were boycotted and professionals—doctors, lawyers, teachers—kept from earning a living. Ordinary workingmen lost their jobs. In many places Tories also lost the right to vote and to be protected by the law, which meant that anyone could harm them without fear of punishment.

Criticism of the Declaration of Independence was not tolerated. Each community had busybodies who eavesdropped on neighbors' conversations and peered through their windows. People who said, or even seemed to be *thinking*, the wrong thing could be fined, forced to pay double taxes, and jailed. Mobs might whip them, tar and feather them, or destroy their property. Many a Tory farmer returned from the fields to find his barn pulled down. One man had to grovel in the mud with a noose around his neck and curse the king. Even the dead weren't allowed to rest. Tory family tombs were sold to raise money for the army, the bodies removed, and the new owners' names carved into the stone. The lead coffin of Sir William Johnson, a hero of the French and Indian War, was melted down for bullets.

The American Revolution became an American tragedy, our first civil war. Tens of thousands of Tories were driven from the land of their birth into exile in England, Canada, and the West Indies. Families split as members cursed each other as scoundrels and traitors. Benjamin Franklin stopped speaking to his Tory son, William, who never spoke to *his* son, William Temple Franklin, a patriot. Fathers fought sons, and there were even cases of relatives killing one another.

Tories fought for the king out of loyalty and to avenge themselves against the rebels. They formed regiments with such names as the Loyal New Englanders, Royal American Regiment of Foot, American Legion, New Jersey Volunteers, and Queen's Loyal Virginians. Tory guerrillas joined the Indians in burning frontier settlements. At one time more Americans were fighting against the Revolution than George Washington had under his command. New York, the most Tory of all the states, gave the king 23,500 troops, but sent only 17,000 to the Continental Army. And it was there, in New York, that Sir William Howe struck next.

AFTER WINNING BOSTON, Washington asked himself what he'd do in the enemy commander's place. Answer: seize New York City, the most important place in the colonies. Besides being the nation's best seaport and a key trading center, New York was a dagger aimed at the centers of rebel power. Guarding the gateway to the Hudson River, it opened

New England to invasion from the west. An army based there could also be brought by sea to Philadelphia, the rebel capital, or to the Southern states.

Washington arrived with his army at the beginning of June 1776. They were not welcomed by the local Tories, who made no secret of their love for the king, and their hope to see the rebels hung sooner, rather than later. New York at that time meant the built-up area at the southern tip of Manhattan Island; the rest was a wild country of low hills, woods, and fields dotted with small farms. Since there were no prepared defenses, Washington did the best he could in a short time. Trenches were dug and breastworks raised along the East River opposite Long Island. An earthen redoubt grandly named Fort Washington sprang up on a hill at the island's northern end. Fort Lee, named for General Charles Lee, one of Washington's officers, was built directly across the Hudson near what is now the New Jersey side of the George Washington Bridge.

On the morning of June 29, lookouts sighted hundreds of sails moving slowly up the Narrows between Staten Island and Long Island. By evening, 130 ships were riding at anchor, rocking in the gentle swells. Sir William Howe had arrived from Halifax.

These ships were only the spearhead of the largest force ever sent from Great Britain. Convoys arrived directly from the mother country during the following weeks, until five hundred vessels filled the Narrows and the Lower Bay. The ships were manned by 10,000 seamen under Admiral Richard "Black Dick" Howe, the general's older brother. They brought 32,000 troops, who were cheered by Tories as they set up their tent cities on Staten Island. Across the harbor, past Bedloe's Island, where the Statue of Liberty now stands, they could see the red roofs of New York.

Not all the invaders were British regulars. Eight thousand of them wore swallow-tailed coats of green or blue and stiff leather hats that made them look like giants. Their hair hung down their backs as far as their waists in braided pigtails.

Many had curled mustaches blackened with the same polish used on their boots. They spoke German and civilians feared them like the devil.

When the Revolution began, British army enlistments were so low that the king had to look elsewhere for fighting men. He looked to Germany, where plenty of troops were available—for a price. Germany was not a united country, but a patchwork of states each having its own prince, government, and army. The smaller states were poor, so their princes turned them into flesh markets in order to raise money. The princes of Brunswick, Waldeck, Anspach, and Hesse made fortunes by renting out their people as soldiers. Since most rented by Britain came from Hesse, all German soldiers-for-hire were called Hessians.

Hessians were military slaves brought to the army during well-organized soldier-catching raids. Farmers were dragged from their fields, shopkeepers from their stores, in handcuffs. Churches were surrounded and the men taken at the end of Sunday services.

The army was hell on earth. The Redcoats' discipline seemed gentle compared to the Hessians'. Sergeants carried heavy canes to beat soldiers for the slightest offense. A poorly sewn button, for example, might bring a fractured skull. Battle-hardened veterans committed suicide rather than face punishment for a serious offense.

The Hessian common soldier gained nothing for his service and suffering. When he went to war, his prince took the rental fee. When he was killed or crippled, his prince received a bounty, but his family saw not a penny. Each corpse brought the prince the equivalent of $22.50. A soldier's only "pay" was what he could steal from the enemy. Yet these men were fierce fighters, made even fiercer by fear, for officers said Americans ate their prisoners. Like the Redcoats, they were masters of the bayonet.

Sir William Howe made his move on August 22, 1776, when the first waves of Redcoats and Hessians landed on Long Island. Long Island is just that, a long island running

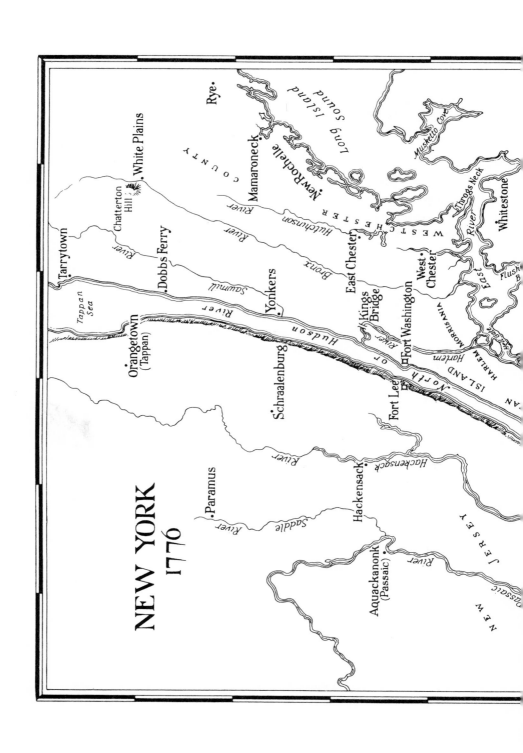

NEW YORK
1776

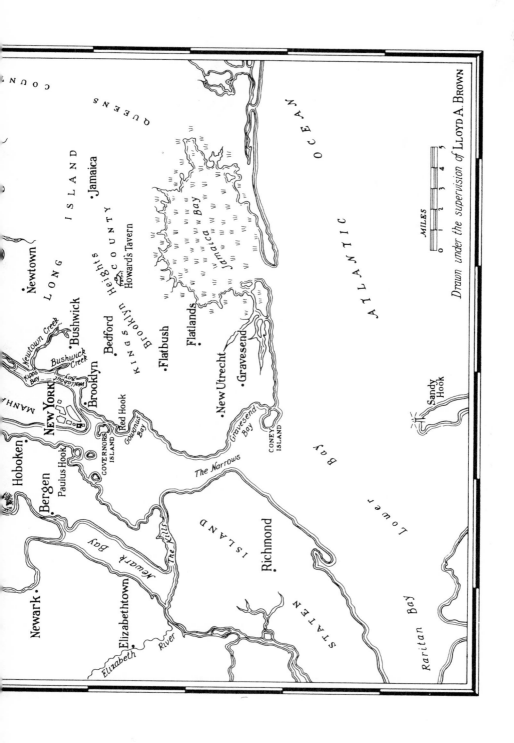

QUEENS COUNTY

LONG ISLAND

JAMAICA

•Jamaica

Bedford Heights

KINGS COUNTY

Howard's Tavern

Jamaica Bay

•Newtown

Bushwick

Newtown Creek

Bushwick Creek

Kipps Bay

Wallabout Bay

•Brooklyn

•Bedford

Brooklyn

•Flatbush

•Flatlands

NEW YORK

Red Hook

Gowanus Bay

•New Utrecht

•Gravesend

GOVERNORS ISLAND

Gravesend Bay

CONEY ISLAND

ATLANTIC OCEAN

Hoboken•

•Bergen

Paulus Hook

The Narrows

Sandy Hook

MANHA

Newark•

Newark Bay

The Kills

STATEN ISLAND

Richmond•

Lower Bay

•Elizabethtown

Elizabeth River

Raritan Bay

Drawn under the supervision of LLOYD A. BROWN

MILES
0  1  2  3  4  5

about 110 miles from east to west. The Americans had two lines of breastworks strung across the western end of the island, an area of marshes near the village of Brooklyn; the name is from *Breukelen,* Dutch for marshland. Their main line rested on Brooklyn Heights overlooking the East River and within cannon range of Manhattan. Their second line was two miles to the east and ran along the crest of a wooded ridge crossed by narrow passes in four places.

Although Washington had only 10,000 men to Howe's 12,000, the Americans were in a strong position and might have done well if not for a stupid error. All the passes were well guarded except for Jamaica Pass on the American left, or the British right. Israel Putnam, commanding on the ridge, did nothing to defend the pass. Perhaps he expected another Bunker Hill, with the British allowing themselves to be slaughtered. Only five sentries were posted at this vital place, which gave access to the American rear from the ridge to Brooklyn Heights.

Meantime Howe wasted precious time. Superiority in men and cannon gave him no comfort. He knew from Bunker Hill how deadly Americans could be from behind breastworks. Days passed, more troops arrived, and still he couldn't bring himself to attack. Then, on the fourth day, a patrol discovered the American weakness.

Once again Howe decided on a right hook followed by a left jab. Sir Henry Clinton would take a strike force through Jamaica Pass into the American rear while the rest of the army hit their left flank, crushing them between walls of steel.

Howe's plan worked like a charm. During the evening of August 26, three Brooklyn Tories led a light infantry detachment through the pass. After silencing the sentries, they signaled Clinton to come forward. During the rest of the night, ten thousand Redcoats moved behind the American positions on the ridge.

The Battle of Long Island began with the new day. At dawn Americans were awakened by musket volleys in their rear. Light cannon roared, filling the air with grape shot. Then came the bayonets. Shouting grenadiers tore through the American line front and rear. The Hessians especially inspired fear wherever they attacked. They surged forward, often pinning Americans to trees with their bayonets.

The American line crumpled as men flung away their weapons and tried to escape to Brooklyn Heights. Hundreds never made it. British cavalrymen with gleaming sabers, curved single-edged swords, galloped among them, cutting them down from behind. Trapped, others fled to the marshes where they drowned. It was a grand hunt, with Americans as the prey. Even women from the British camp joined the chase, capturing scores of terrified Yankees.

George Washington watched the scene from Brooklyn Heights. "Good God!" he cried, wringing his hands. "What brave fellows I must lose this day!" Dismounting from his horse, he walked behind the breastwork with two pistols. There was murder in his eyes as he reminded troops of their duty. Private Hezekiah Munsell always remembered his words: "If I see any man turn his back today, I will shoot him through. . . . I will not ask any man to go further than I do. I will fight so long as I have a leg or an arm."

Despite Washington's threats, his men probably couldn't have held out much longer. Howe's troops could feel victory, and they meant to finish the rebels on the spot. But just then their commander gave Washington an unexpected gift. He halted his advance.

Officers protested. Soldiers, tears in their eyes, begged to go on. But Howe could see once again, this time in his memory, Bunker Hill and British blood streaking his breeches. He repeated his order. Halt the advance! The army must dig in, set up cannon, and blast the rebels off Brooklyn Heights. Never again would he order head-on attacks against entrenched Americans.

Washington used Howe's gift of time to save his army. Luck was with him as thick fog rolled in, forcing Black Dick Howe's warships away from shore and hiding the American

*Disaster at Gowanus Creek. During the Battle of Long Island in August, 1776, Lord William Howe's troops managed to get behind the American lines, causing their defenses to collapse. During the retreat, many Americans were killed in crossing Gowanus Creek. This picture is from a painting by Alonzo Chappell done about 1874.*

positions. He ordered every barge, sailboat, and rowboat in New York to cross the East River. Never mind the poor visibility or the offshore rocks! The Continental Army, America's only army, must be saved whatever the risk.

Among the regiments at Brooklyn were two from Marblehead and Salem, Massachusetts, fishermen with muscular arms and calloused feet who knew the ways of the sea. If anyone could sail in foul weather, it was they.

The fishermen were ordered out of the trenches and into the boats. Then, one by one, the other regiments left the line to be carried through the fog to New York. As each

regiment moved out, weakening the line, its neighbors spread out to the right and left. The evacuation went so smoothly that British sentries a hundred yards away didn't hear a sound. Minutes before daybreak, one of the last Americans out of Brooklyn looked back as his boat left the shore. Through the swirling fog he saw a tall figure in a three-cornered hat and a dark cloak standing on the dock. Like a good ship's captain, General Washington had stayed to the end to make sure that all his men were safe.

It was a small victory, although it could only postpone the final defeat. Manhattan Island had too long a coastline

*Regiments of fishermen from Massachusetts manned the boats in the successful evacuation of Brooklyn.*

to defend and its fortifications were so thin that Black Dick could set his brother's troops ashore almost anywhere. Before dawn of September 15, Private Joseph Plumb Martin was walking his post at Kip's Bay on the East River, just south of the present United Nations building. Martin, a Massachusetts farm boy who'd enlisted at sixteen, was to fight in nearly every major battle of the Revolution. Many years later, as an ailing old man, he described his experiences in a book, *A Narrative of Some of the Adventures, Dangers, and Sufferings of a Revolutionary Soldier.* That book is our best view of the Revolution through the eyes of a common soldier.

Private Martin was making his rounds when, at the half hour, sentries passed the watchword from one post to another: "All is well." Suddenly an Englishman's voice boomed from the blackness, "We will alter your tune before tomorrow night." Black Dick's ships were lurking offshore, invisible, waiting to cover another landing.

At sunrise naval guns ripped into the American breastworks at point-blank range. Clods of earth mingled with pieces of men flew into the air. Washington, hearing the bombardment, rode over to see how things were going. What he saw filled him with anger and shame. Private Martin's comrades, most of them raw militia who'd never been under cannon fire, panicked when the enemy troops landed. Entire regiments, including their officers, ran as if Satan himself was after them. They weren't even trying to defend themselves.

The quiet Virginian went wild. He stormed. He raged. He threw his hat on the ground. He rode in among the troops, flailing about with the flat of his sword. Even his staff officers were frightened. "Good God!" he cried, his voice rising above the confusion. "Are these the men with which I am to defend America?"

They were, and they kept running until they reached the main camp at Harlem Heights, where Columbia University now stands. Since many had lost their packs, and there were few tents, they had to sleep on the bare ground. Fall was in the air. It grew cold and, toward midnight, rain fell in buckets. The lucky ones, too exhausted to feel cold or wet, slept in the mud. The unlucky ones sat up all night with blue lips and chattering teeth. Nobody thought that he'd look back upon this night as one of his better soldiering experiences.

Howe's men lost no time in cutting across the island to the Hudson and capturing New York. During their victory parade down Broadway, Tories flocked to welcome them with cheers and, in the case of some young officers, kisses from pretty girls. The American flag was trampled in the dirt in reprisal for King George's statue. Rebels had celebrated the Declaration of Independence by knocking down the king's statue and molding it into bullets. A large letter *R* was painted on rebel sympathizer's doors, and they went out fearing for their lives.

Howe's troops were jubilant. The defeats at Boston had been wiped away and the rebels made to show their cowardice. Soon the war would be over and they'd be going home.

They learned differently next day, September 16, when the Black Watch, a Scottish Highland regiment and one of the finest in the British army, ran into Thomas Knowlton's Connecticut men on Harlem Heights. Not long before, these veterans of Bunker Hill had also been raw militia. But they'd learned soldiering the only way it can be learned: by hard experience.

When the Black Watch fired, Knowlton's men moved out of range in an orderly fashion. A Scottish bugler, thinking they were running away, sounded the signal hunters use when chasing a fox. That was a mistake. Knowlton's men turned and opened fire on the kilted warriors. Washington, a old fox-hunter himself, also heard the bugle. Then and there he vowed to teach these arrogant Britishers a lesson. Troops were sent to support Knowlton, and this time they obeyed. Hessians soon joined in on the British side as well.

Americans stood up to the enemy and slugged it out with them hour after hour, until the British decided that they'd had enough for one day. This Battle of Harlem Heights surprised both sides. For the first time Americans had met European professionals in open battle and made them turn tail. And what they had done once, they could do again. Hessian prisoners were amazed that their captors had no intention of eating them. In time word that Americans were really quite civilized reached their comrades, encouraging thousands to desert and settle in the United States. We know that 29,166 German soldiers came to America, of whom over 12,000, or over 40 percent, never returned to their homeland.

Although the British had their city, some New Yorkers

decided they shouldn't enjoy it. Shortly after midnight, September 20, Washington's army on Harlem Heights saw a red glow in the south. It grew brighter and spread as the lower end of Manhattan Island, near the site of today's World Trade Center's towers, became a sea of flame. British soldiers sent to fight the blaze found pumps broken and the handles of water buckets cut. Men were found in several houses with torches or actually starting fires. They were instantly killed by the angry soldiers and their bodies thrown into the flames. By the time the fire was put out; over five hundred buildings, one-fifth of the city, lay in ashes.

The British accused Washington of arson, but he denied the charge and they had no proof. Not that it saddened him to see the Tory stronghold burn. "Providence, or some good honest fellow," he said, "has done more for us than we were disposed to do for ourselves." Little did he know that one day he'd take the oath of office as first president of the United States in that city.

Washington realized that he was vulnerable to British sea power as long as he remained on Manhattan Island. All Howe had to do was set troops down on the mainland to the north and the Americans would be trapped. To prevent this, Washington decided to withdraw across King's Bridge at the island's northern tip, leaving behind a garrison at Fort Washington to cover his retreat.

The evacuation was completed when, late in October, Howe sent a fleet up the East River into Long Island Sound and landed troops in Westchester County, New York. He caught up with the Americans at White Plains.

By now British officers were calling Washington the Old Fox because, like a sly old fox, he always managed to escape at the last moment. Although defeated in the all-day Battle of White Plains, he withdrew before the enemy could drive in for the kill. A few days later he crossed the Hudson into New Jersey. Howe returned to Manhattan to deal with Fort Washington.

The only resemblance between Fort Washington and a

*Fort Washington was the last American position on Manhattan Island after the British captured New York City. Poorly constructed and overcrowded, it was taken in a combined assault by British Redcoats and Hessian mercenaries. This view of Washington Heights from across the Harlem River was drawn on the spot by Thomas Davis, a British artillery captain.*

real fort was its name. Little more than a redoubt set on a hill overlooking the Hudson, it had no buildings, no protective ditch, no water supply inside its walls; water had to be brought up a steep cliff in buckets. The place invited attack.

On November 17, warships opened a terrific bombardment from the Hudson and Harlem rivers. Solid shot tore away chunks of wall. Shells, hollow balls filled with gunpowder and detonated by fuses, hissed and sputtered until they exploded with a deafening roar. The hero of the bombardment was a little spotted dog that seemed to belong to nobody.

The dog would watch for a shell to land, place his front paws on it, catch the fuse in his teeth, and pull it out. Soldiers cheered their little lifesaver until a shell exploded and he vanished in a flash of light.

Hessian grenadiers rushed the gate, followed by thousands of Redcoats. After a short, sharp fight, the Americans began surrendering in droves. No sooner did they raise their hands when Hessians began robbing them of even the clothes off their backs. They would have left them stark naked had not British officers interceded.

Redcoats marched the prisoners to New York City, where they were met by mobs of women from the British camp who thought the American commander in chief had been captured. "Which is Washington? Which is Washington?" they shouted. Only a hedgehog of bayonets kept them from the prisoners. Had Washington fallen into their hands, they would have torn him to bits.

*After the capture of Fort Washington, British forces crossed the Hudson River and climbed the Palisades to attack Fort Lee in November, 1776. This was also painted by Thomas Davis.*

Howe sent Lord Charles Cornwallis to take Fort Lee two days later. Cornwallis crossed the Hudson, where he was met by a Tory who guided his force to the top of the Palisades, the rugged cliffs that line the New Jersey side of the river. Fortunately, Fort Lee had been abandoned, although in such haste that the Redcoats found the garrison's breakfast bubbling in kettles.

"I feel mad, sick and sorry," said General Nathanael Greene, one of Washington's most trusted aides. In eleven weeks the patriots had lost Long Island, New York City, and much of Westchester County. Forts Washington and Lee had cost them nearly three thousand dead and captured, plus thousands of muskets and countless tons of other supplies. Nothing remained now but to retreat across New Jersey, just ahead of Lord Cornwallis's army.

Washington's retreat brought the evils of war to New Jersey. After the Continentals passed through an area, Tories, feeling safe at last, turned on their neighbors. New Jersey patriots suffered as Tory bands roamed the countryside, meting out their own brand of justice with torch, rope, and gun. They were helped by Redcoats and Hessians, who moved across the land like a plague of locusts, ransacking homes and stealing whatever could be stuffed into knapsacks.

Lord Cornwallis didn't like such doings, although he thought they might provoke Washington into making a mistake. His inability to protect his own people was proof of Washington's weakness. Cornwallis hoped that his pride would be so hurt that he'd turn to fight him in a last, desperate winner-take-all battle.

Yet that is exactly what he would never do. Washington was a person who learned easily from his mistakes. If one approach to a problem failed, he was man enough to admit his errors and look for a better way. His defeats in New York had taught him that the Continental Army itself was more important than winning a certain battle or holding a certain piece of territory. *The army was the Revolution.* As long as it existed, Britain was defied and the Revolution lived. Wherever it camped, there was a corner of free America. This understanding guided the commander in chief for the rest of the war. He would retreat, bide his time, and hit back when the enemy gave him an opening. But he would never risk the army's destruction, for fear of destroying the Revolution along with it.

Retreat became a monotonous routine. As the Americans passed, their rear guard slowed their pursuers as best they could. Axmen felled trees along the line of march. Each time a stream was crossed, bridges were burned and boats sunk.

The army marched southward throughout November and December of 1776, crossing one New Jersey river after another. First it crossed the Passaic, then the Rahway, the Raritan and the Millstone, always just a step ahead of Cornwal-

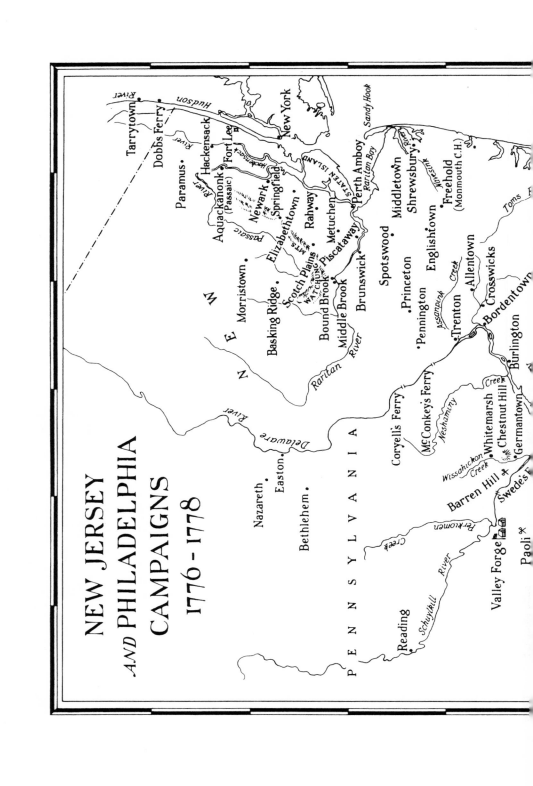

NEW JERSEY
AND PHILADELPHIA
CAMPAIGNS
1776 – 1778

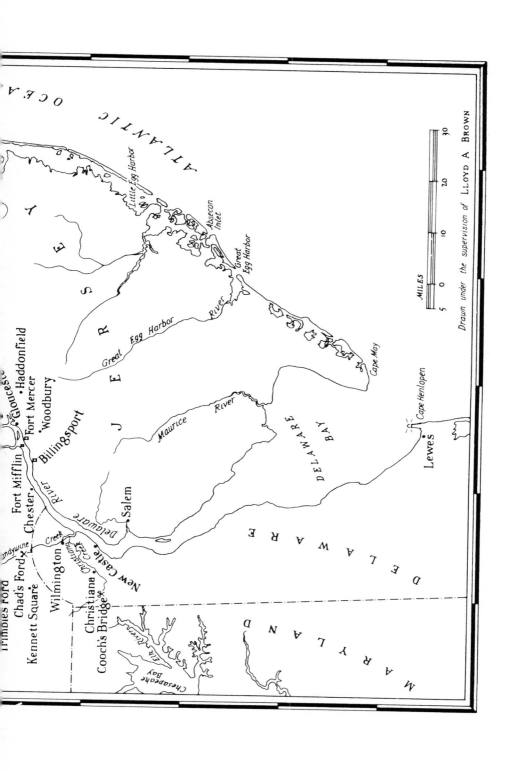

ATLANTIC OCEAN

Little Egg Harbor

Absecon Inlet

Great Egg Harbor

Great Egg Harbor River

Cape May

NEW JERSEY

Maurice River

Gloucester
Haddonfield
Fort Mercer
Woodbury
Billingsport
Fort Mifflin
Chester
Delaware River
Trimbles Ford
Chads Ford
Kennett Square
Brandywine
Wilmington
Christiana
Cooch's Bridge
Christiana Creek
New Castle
Salem

DELAWARE BAY

Cape Henlopen
Lewes

DELAWARE

MARYLAND

Chesapeake Bay
Elk River

MILES
5   0   10   20   30

Drawn under the supervision of LLOYD A. BROWN

lis's columns. As it neared the Delaware, the border between New Jersey and Pennsylvania, Congress fled from Philadelphia to Baltimore, Maryland, "the dirtiest city in the world," according to John Adams.

Washington's troops suffered terribly during the retreat. More were put out of action by rain and mud than by British bullets. Hundreds had no stockings, so that wet feet constantly rubbed against wet shoe leather. The result was "scald feet," swelling that felt as if you'd been standing for hours in boiling water.

At least these men had shoes. Shoes that had been new in the spring were shapeless, holey chunks of leather by autumn. Soldiers walked barefoot or wrapped their feet in dirty rags. It was the same with coats and shirts, breeches, hats and underwear: One did without or wore rags.

Hunger gnawed at soldiers' guts. The Continental Army's quartermaster department was always behind in food deliveries; and when food did arrive, it was never enough or of good quality. Private Martin felt lucky to get a fresh sheep's head, "all the provisions I had for two or three days." Usually, however, meat was rotten. Salt to mask the taste was as precious as gold, and soldiers filled their pockets with it whenever any came their way. The rest of their diet consisted of dried peas hard as bullets and stale, moldy bread.

Wagons occasionally met the marching columns with barrels of whiskey. Whiskey was as necessary to the soldier's well-being as any other "food." Its alcohol warmed him against the cold, dulled his aches and pains, and cheered him when he felt gloomy. No wonder his jolliest songs were drinking songs. No wonder, too, that many men became drunkards in the army.

The retreating soldiers were glad to have a roof over their heads after a day's march. Still, it wasn't pleasant to sleep in stables or outhouses, the outdoor toilets. The odor was awful to all but the soldiers themselves. Not having washed for weeks, they stank of sweat and dirt. But since everyone stank alike, no one noticed after a while.

Private Martin wrote movingly about being without that most simple of luxuries—a bed:

> How many times have I had to lie down like a dumb animal in the field, and hear "the pelting of the pitiless storm," cruel enough in warm weather, but how much more so in the heart of winter. Could I have had the benefit of a little fire, it would have been deemed a luxury. But when snow or rain would fall so heavy that it was impossible to keep a spark alive, to have to weather out a long, wet, cold, tedious night in the depth of winter, with scarcely clothes enough to keep one from freezing instantly, how discouraging it must be, I leave to my reader to judge.
>
> It is fatiguing, almost beyond belief, to those that never experienced it, to be obliged to march twenty-four or forty-eight hours . . . and often more, night and day without rest or sleep, wishing and hoping that some wood or village I could see ahead might prove a short resting place, when, alas, I came to it, almost tired off my legs, it proved no resting place for me. *How often have I envied the very swine their happiness*, when I have heard them quarreling in their warm dry sties, when I was wet to the skin and wished for that indulgence. And even in dry warm weather, I have often been so beat out with long and tedious marching that I have fallen asleep while walking the road and not been sensible of it till I have jostled against someone in the same situation; and when permitted to stop and have the . . . happiness to roll myself in my blanket and drop down on the ground in the bushes, briars, thorns, or thistles, and get an hour or two's sleep. Oh! how exhilarating.

At last the Continental Army crossed the Delaware into Pennsylvania. It crossed at night, with mist clinging to leafless trees glistening with ice. Blazing bonfires lit the landing sites for the boats along the shore. Cannon and wagons creaked past the fires, pulled by bony horses. Shadowy figures emerged for a moment, coughing and swearing, only to be swallowed up again by the darkness. Lieutenant Charles Willson Peale was watching the procession from the riverbank when a soldier staggered out of line and came toward him. "He had lost all his clothes. He was in an old dirty blanket-jacket, his beard long and his face full of sores. He could not clean it, which so disfigured him that he was not known to me at first sight. Only when he spoke did I recognize my brother James."

The Continental Army was a wreck. Washington, who also watched from the riverbank, was so sad that he wrote his brother, John Augustine, "I think the game is pretty near up."

Sir William Howe agreed. A few days earlier, he'd sent the British army into winter quarters in New York. Lord Cornwallis was to give up the chase and have the Hessians set up outposts to prevent Washington's recrossing the Delaware. Not that he expected such boldness. The Continental Army was so weak that he would let the winter save him the bother of finishing it off. There would be time enough in the spring to hunt down the survivors and hang those rascals in Congress.

NOW, with the enemy snug in winter quarters, Washington stopped running. His target was Trenton on the Delaware, with fifteen hundred troops the main Hessian outpost in New Jersey. The attack was set for Christmas night, December 25–26, when most of the Hessians would be drunk or exhausted from the day's celebrations.

About twenty-four hundred Continentals began marching toward the Pennsylvania side of McKonkey's Ferry several miles upstream from Trenton late on Christmas afternoon.

Paths down to the river were covered with snow. In the failing light, Washington saw the snow marked by the bloody footprints of those who went without shoes. None complained; it wouldn't have done any good.

It hadn't been a merry Christmas for those gathered on the shore. Miserable and homesick, they stood about in groups, waiting to board the boats. Rain began to fall, then wet snow. The temperature dropped. All they had to cheer them were the words of Tom Paine's latest pamphlet, printed in Philadelphia three days earlier.

Paine had marched with the army, sharing its hardships, since Fort Lee. That experience inspired him. At night he'd sit by a campfire with a drum between his knees. Using the drumhead as a desk, he wrote *The American Crisis.*

As the shivering troops waited, Washington had the pamphlet read to them. Paine's words went to their hearts like flaming arrows. "These are the times that try men's souls. The summer soldier and the sunshine patriot will, in this crisis, shrink from the service of their country, but he who stands it *now,* deserves the love and thanks of men and women. Tyranny, like hell, is not easily conquered; yet we have this consolation with us, that the harder the conflict, the more glorious the triumph. . . ."

Ragged men looked at each other and nodded agreement. Paine had given words to feelings that all shared but couldn't express for themselves. They were not summer soldiers, sunshine patriots. Nor were they professionals drilled to perform as robots. They were a new force in the world: citizen-soldiers who fought for a cause they believed made life worth living. For that they willingly suffered terrible hardships.

The boats cast off about 11 P.M. It was a rough passage even though the same Massachusetts fishermen who'd taken the army from Brooklyn manned the oars. Snow began falling heavily and the wind made the flakes hiss as they struck men's faces. Large blocks of ice bobbed in the swift current, grinding against the boats' sides. The passengers sucked in

*On Christmas Eve, 1776, George Washington led his army across the
icy Delaware River to attack the Hessians at Trenton. This painting
by the German Emanuel Leutze is inaccurate in at least two details.
Washington may not have been a sailor, but he was smart enough not
to stand in a boat during a dangerous river crossing. Moreover, the
Americans had no flag of their own at this time.*

their breath, hoping they wouldn't have to swim the rest of
the way.

Washington crossed with the lead boats. A soldier recalled
that his nose had turned cherry-red in the wind and that
"He was not what the ladies would call a pretty man." His

boat bounced and lurched, its sides dipping dangerously into the water. Henry Knox—all three hundred pounds of him—sat in the stern, throwing it off balance. The general cupped his hands to his mouth, shouting: "Shift your tail, Knox, and trim the boat!"

Once ashore, the army assembled in marching order and started for its objective. Nearing Trenton, Washington divided it into three columns. At 8 A.M. sharp, they struck from different directions.

Surprise was total. The first sign of trouble was the crackling of gunfire and laughter. Peering from their windows, Hessians saw Americans running through the streets, laughing and shouting, "These are the times that try men's souls!"

The Hessians, groggy from their celebrations, recovered enough to put up a good fight. But not good enough. After two hours they surrendered, having lost 22 killed, 92 wounded, and 948 captured; their attackers had 2 wounded and none killed. That night Washington's army recrossed the Delaware with its captives. Despite the Americans' hunger, Hessians noted in letters home that not a single captive was eaten.

Encouraged by his success, Washington decided to go after other enemy outposts in New Jersey. There was just one problem: With the year ending, the enlistments of all but a few of his men were due to expire. Now, Washington wasn't an easygoing person. Words didn't come to him readily, and public speaking made him uncomfortable. Yet he had to persuade the troops to sign up for at least a few more weeks or cancel his plan, which would have amounted to another defeat.

On December 31, drums beat and troops fell into ranks. It was the last day of their enlistments and they were glad. Although they loved their country, they were sick and tired of war. Let others take their places, they thought. They wanted to go home.

Washington faced them on horseback. He spoke of Trenton and told them that some more fighting was necessary before going into winter quarters. To encourage them to sign up, he offered a $10 bounty in addition to their regular pay.

Again drums beat, inviting volunteers to "make their mark," to sign up. No one moved. They just stood at attention, staring ahead.

Suddenly Washington understood. They had been through too much to be bribed with a few extra dollars. Again he spoke, only this time from the heart. "My brave fellows," he said, "you have done all I asked you to do, and more than could reasonably be expected. But your country is at stake, your wives, your houses, and all that you hold dear. You have worn yourselves out with fatigues and hardships, but we know not how to spare you."

Something in his voice touched those ragged scarecrows. The general had swallowed his pride to beg them to do their duty. Embarrassed, they glanced at each other sideways, not letting their eyes meet. "I will remain if you will," one muttered. "We cannot go home under such circumstances," echoed another. By ones and twos, then by scores and hundreds, they stepped forward to sign.

Private Samuel Downing, when he was 109 years old, explained the common soldier's attitude toward Washington. "Oh! but you never got a smile out of him. He was a nice man. *We loved him.* They'd sell their lives for him." Their love for him grew, not in happy times, but in the times that tried men's souls.

Washington recrossed the Delaware, only to be cornered by Lord Cornwallis at Assunpink Creek east of Trenton, January 2, 1777. But since darkness was falling, and he wanted to rest his troops, Cornwallis postponed the attack. "We've got the old fox now," he said. "We'll go over and bag him in the morning."

The new day dawned clear and cold. And quiet. No sound came from the American lines. Inching forward, British scouts found only smoldering campfires. The Old Fox had given them the slip again. Under cover of darkness,

*George Washington leads his troops at the Battle of Princeton. After escaping a British trap the night before, the Americans caught the enemy in a surprise attack outside the college town on January 3, 1777.*

he'd led his army out of the trap by way of a little-used trail.

Cornwallis learned Washington's destination when messengers arrived from Princeton to the north. Two British regiments had been on their way to join the main army in Princeton when Washington struck. Spurring his horse forward, he led the charge personally. Instantly the field was enveloped in the fog of battle. When the smoke cleared, Washington stood in his stirrups and shouted, "It is a fine fox chase, my boys!" The British ran for their lives, while the Continentals dashed into Princeton. There they found a supply dump with hundreds of barrels of flour and piles of tents, blankets, and shoes.

Sir William Howe had had enough of winter fighting. He ordered Cornwallis to abandon all New Jersey outposts except Perth Amboy and New Brunswick. Washington, now in control of most of the state, led his army into winter quarters in the hills around Morristown.

A short time later, an English traveler wrote from Virginia that people "are liberty mad" again. Washington's victories at Trenton and Princeton revived patriots' spirits and convinced the British that they were in for a long war. Had Washington failed in New Jersey, the American Revolution would have failed. But by winning at the last moment, he gave the United States a chance to survive.

# · FOUR ·

# The Turning Point

KING George III and his advisers knew that 1777 would be a very important year. The American Revolution had by then stirred Europe's imagination with its ideas of liberty and national independence. Already scores of foreign officers had come seeking commissions in the Continental Army. Some, like Thaddeus Kosciuszko and Count Casimir Pulaski, whose native Poland was being torn apart by its neighbors, saw America's struggle as their own. Others, like the German Baron Johann de Kalb, were professional soldiers eager for promotion and a chance to follow their only trade.

The largest number of volunteers were Frenchmen, among them a pudgy, red-haired fellow with a long, pointed nose. His name was Marie Joseph Paul Yves Roch Gilbert de Motier, Marquis de Lafayette. Older men called him "The Boy" behind his back, as he was only nineteen when he arrived. Yet they said it warmly, for although a wealthy nobleman, he'd adopted America as his second homeland. "The moment I heard of America," he said, "I loved her. The moment I knew she was fighting for freedom, I burned with a desire of bleeding for her."

*The French Marquis de Lafayette was the most famous of the many Europeans who came to aid the Americans during their Revolution.*

Lafayette's master, King Louis XVI, was becoming a problem for Great Britain. Not only did he allow his subjects to fight for America, he though the rebel cause might serve France's national interests. King Louis saw the Revolution as a low-risk way of avenging his country's defeat in the French and Indian War. He decided to aid the rebels in every way short of war. If they failed, he'd simply write off the cost as a bad investment. But if they seemed to be winning, he'd enter the war, defeat Britain, and regain at least some of his lost territories.

For the time being, Louis XVI was satisfied to aid the rebels secretly. A dummy trading company was set up to trade with the islands of the French West Indies. But instead of cargoes of wine and cheese, the company's ships carried guns, ammunition, and medical supplies. When the ships reached port, their cargoes were transferred to waiting American vessels. In this way the Continental Army received over 80 percent of its gunpowder.

British spies, however, kept London well informed of these goings on. British war planners soon realized that the rebels must be crushed quickly or Britain risked war with France, a major power with allies such as Spain.

As winter gave way to spring and the trees around Morristown blossomed, Washington became puzzled about Sir William Howe's lack of activity. The British commander sat with his army in New York City doing, it seemed, absolutely nothing. Why? Washington wondered and worried.

Meantime, Britain prepared her knockout blow. The war planners had devised a two-part scheme to finish the war within a few months. The first part of their scheme called for Howe to use most of his force against Washington. They believed that he'd have to fight for Philadelphia, the American capital. What they didn't understand was that America, unlike a European country, had no real capital because it had no central government. Until the Constitution was adopted in 1787, Congress could make no laws or force the states to do anything. At best, it issued nearly worthless paper money to pay for the war, appointed military and naval officers, and sent representatives to foreign governments. Thus, America's "capital" was wherever Congress happened to be. In any case, Howe would go for Philadelphia, destroy Washington's army, and then conquer the rest of Pennsylvania, New Jersey, and Delaware. At the same time Gentleman Johnny Burgoyne was to lead a large army southward from Canada to Albany, New York, and link up with a smaller force that had advanced up the Hudson from New York City. With Howe victorious and New England cut off from the rest of the country, the rebellion would collapse.

Washington's suspense ended on July 20, when he learned that a British fleet had sailed from New York the day before. Howe had put to sea with 260 ships and seventeen hundred soldiers. The fleet headed south, which meant its destination was Philadelphia. Immediately the Americans broke camp and moved to block the city's southern approaches.

They needn't have hurried, for what would normally have been a week's voyage turned into a month-long ordeal for the British. Once at sea, the wind died down, becalming the fleet in hundred-degree temperatures. The vessels stank of melting tar, rotting food, and unwashed bodies. Horses, cramped belowdecks, went mad in the heat and had to be shot. Then came thunderstorms. Masts were split by lightning and sails torn to shreds. Finally the fleet anchored off Head of Elk, Maryland, on Chesapeake Bay, fifty miles south of Philadelphia, August 25, 1777.

The armies met at Brandywine Creek, twenty-five miles from the City of Brotherly Love. The Brandywine flowed between steep banks and was difficult to cross except at shallow places called "fords." At the best of these, Chadds Ford, Washington placed his best troops and most of his artillery. The next move was up to the enemy.

Howe would not risk a frontal assault across a wide stream. On September 11, while Hessians opened fire to keep the Americans busy at Chadds Ford, he sent Lord Cornwallis to cross upstream, out of sight, and hit their right flank.

The maneuver worked beautifully. A fierce battle began, and a losing one for the Americans, who steadily gave ground to avoid being encircled. They suffered over twelve hundred casualties and left so many wounded behind that Howe asked Washington to send surgeons to treat them.

The commander in chief had a close call himself that day. British Major Patrick Ferguson, nicknamed "Bull Dog," was resting with some men in a clump of trees when a party of American officers rode past without seeing them. One of Ferguson's men happened to have a rifle of the major's design, as fine a weapon as any frontiersman's. A crack shot, he aimed at the easiest target, the back of the biggest man on the biggest horse. He was squeezing the trigger when the major, who thought it ungentlemanly to shoot a fellow officer from hiding, motioned for him to lower the gun. Next day Ferguson learned from an American prisoner that the officer was George Washington. "I am not sorry that I did not know at the time who he was," he said, relieved. Not knowing made it unnecessary to choose between doing something he thought dishonorable and possibly ending the war by killing the enemy commander.

The Boy—Lafayette—didn't get away so easily. Although shot in the leg, he didn't notice the wound until his boot filled with blood. A surgeon was patching him up when Washington rode into camp. Lafayette smiled and joked about the mess. Washington, unamused, snapped an order to the surgeon: "Treat him as if he were my son, for I love him as if he were." In his mind the young Frenchman represented the son he never had.

History had repeated itself. Once again Howe had outmaneuvered Washington. But, once again the Old Fox had given him the slip and saved his army. And once again the Americans lost a major city. On September 26, a week after Congress fled to York, Pennsylvania, Howe occupied Philadelphia. Yet nothing seemed to have changed. The Americans, to Howe's amazement, didn't know they were supposed to collapse after losing their "capital." Instead, they attacked.

After occupying Philadelphia, Howe set up his main camp at Germantown, north of the city. Washington quickly saw a chance to repeat his surprise at Trenton. Four columns of troops were ordered to move at night by different roads. At dawn, October 4, they were to close in like the jaws of a bear trap.

The Battle of Germantown turned out to be a comedy of errors—of *deadly* errors. Two of Washington's columns got lost and missed the battle altogether. The first column to arrive on the scene surprised Howe's light infantry, sending them fleeing in panic. Several of the light infantry companies, however, took shelter in Chew House, a large two-story building with walls a foot thick.

Chew House shouldn't have been a problem. All Washington needed to do was leave a few hundred men to pin down the British while the rest of the column pressed the assault. Unfortunately, he listened to Henry Knox, who wanted to stall the attack until his artillery had forced the defenders to surrender.

Knox was a good officer, but he still had a lot to learn. His cannon fired six-pounders, which bounced off the walls like Ping-Pong balls. Whenever troops tried to rush the house, the Redcoats shot them down. Within a half-hour, fifty American bodies were piled before the door or sprawled in the front yard. At last Washington ordered a guard to remain at Chew House while the rest of the column pushed ahead. Too late.

It was foggy that morning, and the fog, mixed with gunsmoke, often made it difficult to see more than a few yards ahead. As the column advanced, the second column arrived and, mistaking it for the enemy, opened fire. War is full of accidents, especially "friendly fire," being shot at by one's own side. The result was such a bloody mix-up, with Americans killing Americans, that Howe was able to rally his troops

*The Battle of Germantown, October 4, 1777, might well have been an American victory had they not wasted time trying to dislodge British troops defending Chew House, a fortlike mansion with thick walls.*

for a counterattack. Germantown cost the Continental Army eleven hundred killed, wounded, and captured.

Despite their defeat, the Americans weren't down-hearted. Their spirits actually improved, for they thought they'd almost won. Bad luck, not bad planning, accounted for the foul-up. Next time, they promised themselves, they'd do better.

Germantown gave Sir William Howe a scare. He expected easy victories after taking Philadelphia, but clearly the Old Fox still had plenty of fight in him. Instead of continuing his offensive, Howe began to fortify Philadelphia against an American attack. Washington camped nearby at Whitemarsh. His troops were worn out, hungry, and in no condition to fight another battle soon. Although he'd try to block any British advance into the countryside, he hoped they'd sit tight in Philadelphia. He, like Howe, had done enough fighting for 1777.

Suddenly, in mid-October, every cannon in the American camp roared. Howe did nothing, for he knew they were being fired not in anger, but in joy. An express rider had just come with a message from New York City: Gentleman Johnny Burgoyne and his entire army had surrendered at Saratoga in New York. The American Revolution had reached its turning point.

BURGOYNE left Canada in June 1777, a month before Howe sailed from New York. His army numbered ninety-five hundred British and Hessian regulars, plus another thousand Tories and Indians, mostly Wyandots and Ottawas from near the Great Lakes. There were also hundreds of women and children, among them the family of Baron Adolf von Riedesel, the German commander. His wife, Frederike, carried with her their three small daughters and three nurses. An educated woman, she kept a diary that contains exciting descriptions of everyday life during the campaign.

Gentleman Johnny selected a route that went most of the way by water, the best means of moving heavy baggage and artillery in the wilderness. His route lay across Lake Champlain to Lake George, then overland a few miles to the Hudson River and Albany on its west bank.

An armada of barges towed by sailing craft glided across Lake Champlain. It was glorious July weather, and the expedition moved easily under a cloudless sky. The lake blazed with color, reflecting the scarlet and blue of uniforms, the green of Tory scouts' jackets, and the Indians' war paint. Braves painted themselves from head to toe in solid colors, or stripes and circles, zigzags and splashes, of all the colors of the rainbow. Many had shaven heads, smooth except for a center tuft, or "roach," stiffened with bear grease and crowned with turkey feathers. Stuck through their noses were strands of silver wire dangling coins with the image of King George III. Now and then women stared in disbelief at a brave with a necklace made of the dried fingers of enemies long dead.

The expedition met little opposition at first. General Philip Schuyler, the American commander in New York State, had forty-five hundred men to defend a vast area. The first he knew that the enemy was near was a report of Redcoats swarming ashore near Fort Ticonderoga. Fort Ti had been neglected since its capture by Ethan Allen. Its best guns had been taken for the siege of Boston, and its walls were crumbling in places. Soldiers called it Golgotha, after the Biblical Place of Skulls; its grounds were stuffed with bodies buried in the last war, so that trenches couldn't be dug without uncovering human remains. According to General "Mad" Anthony Wayne, one of Washington's best field commanders, diggers lacking cups drank from skulls. Shin and thigh bones made fine tent pegs.

Ti's greatest problem, however, lay outside the walls. Mount Defiance, a half-mile to the south, overlooked the fort. But since it seemed unlikely that cannon could be brought up its steep slopes, Mount Defiance was undefended.

Gentleman Johnny's engineers knew better. On the nights of July 3 and 4, they cut a trail and hauled up their guns, forcing the Americans to abandon Fort Ticonderoga without a shot. Baron von Riedesel and Brigadier General Simon Fraser, who led the advance troops, chased them as far as Skenesborough near the New York–Vermont border.

Burgoyne now made his first mistake, and it was a whopper. Instead of returning to Ti to continue the advance by water, he decided to march straight to the east bank of the

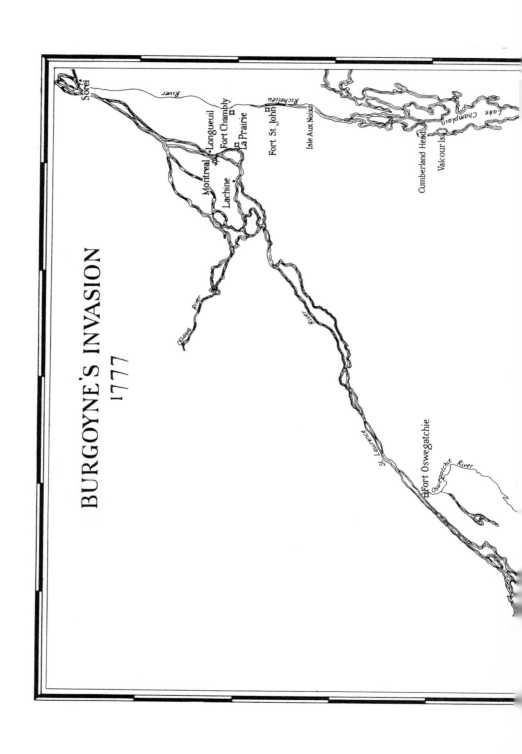

BURGOYNE'S INVASION
1777

Sorel

Ottawa River

Montreal
Lachine
Longueuil
Fort Chambly
La Prairie
Fort St. John
Isle Aux Noix
Richelieu River

St. Lawrence River

Fort Oswegatchie
Oswegatchie River

Cumberland Head
Valcour Is.
Lake Champlain

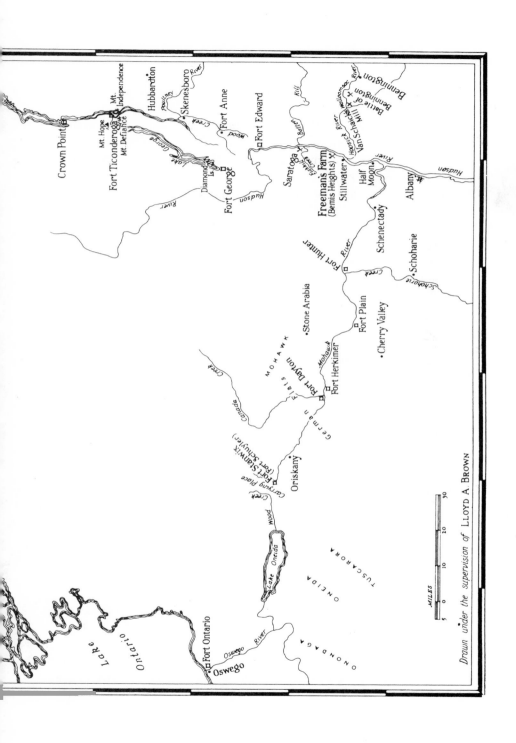

Drawn under the supervision of LLOYD A. BROWN

Hudson and cross above Albany. Ahead of him lay twenty-three miles of rough country made even rougher by the Americans. General Schuyler's axmen felled thousands of trees and interlaced their sharpened branches to form crude "barbed wire" entanglements. Boulders were rolled into creeks to make them overflow and trenches dug to carry swamps over dry land.

Burgoyne's advance slowed to a crawl. Men clothed in wool worked up to their chests in ooze and slime to build forty bridges; that is, one bridge per half-mile. Mosquitoes and "punkies," tiny beasts with bites like electric needles, rose from the swamps in clouds to torture the sweating men. Finally, after moving as little as a mile a day, Burgoyne reached the Hudson on July 29.

George Washington, busy with his own problems in New Jersey, did what he could to help. He sent troops from New York under Major General Benedict Arnold north. Arnold was lame but as ready to fight as ever. Colonel Daniel Morgan arrived with five hundred Virginia, Maryland, and Pennsylvania riflemen. Morgan, a quiet giant with a ready smile, hated the British. "Count 'em," he'd say, raising his shirt to show the five hundred scars on his back. He'd hit a brutal officer during the French and Indian War and had been whipped until his back was a mass of hideous welts. Then and there he promised to make the British pay for every welt on his back.

Schuyler's main reinforcements, however, were militiamen, and they had a score to settle. As Burgoyne's army had neared the Hudson, Wyandot scouts found two women alone in a house. The older was the Widow McNeil, a bad-tempered Tory lady who demanded to be taken to General Simon Fraser, her cousin. The other woman, also a Tory, was Jane McCrea, a golden-haired beauty of twenty-three.

The captives were separated and the Widow McNeil was hurried along ahead of Jane. All went well until Jane's captors began arguing about who should claim credit for her capture. Suddenly a brave named Wyandot Panther ended the argu-

*General "Gentleman Johnny" Burgoyne surrendered his entire army at Saratoga in New York State.*

ment. He shot Jane and, leaning over her body, drew a knife from his belt. Holding her hair with one hand, he cut a circle around the hairline and pulled.

When Wyandot Panther rode into camp, Widow McNeil immediately recognized the bloody scalp dangling from his belt. So did Lieutenant David Jones, a Tory Jane was engaged to marry. Gentleman Johnny sentenced Wyandot Panther to hang for murder, then freed him for fear of losing his Indian allies. He was being practical, not just, and so lost everyone's respect. The Indians, insulted at the brave's treatment by the white chief, left a few days later.

Americans were outraged. Not that there was anything unusual about Indians murdering settlers; the day Jane died, July 27, a farmer, his wife, three children, and three blacks were killed nearby. But Jane was a Tory, and that made all the difference. For if the king's supporters weren't safe from Burgoyne's Indians, people could imagine what would happen to patriots if he won.

As Jane's story spread through New York and New England, thousands of men reached for their muskets and set out to "git" Burgoyne. Among them was John Stark, the hero of the rail fence at Bunker Hill and now a general in the New Hampshire militia. Within a week, two thousand men, including the Green Mountain Boys, were gathered at Bennington, Vermont, a large rebel supply base. Stark sensed trouble and he was right.

Burgoyne's army had been weakened by its overland march. Food was becoming scarce. The Hessian cavalry, dressed in stiff leather breeches and boots that weighed twelve pounds a pair, lacked horses. Gentleman Johnny ordered Colonel Friedrich Baum to take 650 men—Hessians, Tories, and a company of Redcoats—and steal whatever they could at Bennington.

August 16, 1777, found the raiders camped on a low hill outside town. Stark held his main force in reserve while others surrounded the hill and worked their way between the German outposts. Colonel Baum could easily have scattered them with his field guns, but he did nothing. He spoke no English and may have thought his visitors were Tories come to welcome him. Besides, they seemed harmless, dressed as they were in work clothes and carrying ancient guns of every type. Then they opened fire at close range.

The shooting was Stark's signal to send his main force into action. "There they are, men!" he shouted, pointing

*At the Battle of Bennington in present-day southern Vermont,*
*American General John Stark, seen on horseback in the center of the*
*picture, surprised a Hessian force sent to gather supplies. As a result*
*of the battle, August 16, 1777, the Hessians lost eight hundred men,*
*another serious setback to British General "Gentlemen Johnny"*
*Burgoyne on his way to Saratoga.*

up the hill. "We'll beat them before night, or Molly Stark will be a widow!"

The Americans raced in from all sides. The Germans held their ground until their ammunition ran out, then they tried to cut their way out with sabers. But when Colonel Baum fell with a bullet in the brain, they surrendered. A relief party that arrived soon afterward had the same reception. Altogether, Bennington cost Burgoyne 207 killed and 700 captured, compared to 30 American dead and 4 wounded.

The Americans were not generous in victory. Enemy regulars were treated as prisoners of war, Tories as traitors. People jeered as they were pushed along through Bennington on their way to jail or, worse, to the abandoned Simsbury copper mines in Connecticut, where men lived underground for years without seeing daylight. A veteran remembered years later how he'd led one Tory with his left eye shot out on a horse who had also lost its left eye. "It seems to me cruel now—but it did not then," he said.

Another British defeat was brewing at that very moment a hundred miles to the west. Besides Burgoyne's own advance, a two-thousand-man army under Colonel Barry St. Leger had been sent along the Mohawk River, which joins the Hudson a few miles above Albany. Local people called it the Bloody Mohawk. For nearly a century, French and Indian raiders from Canada had paddled their canoes across Lake Ontario to enter the river and terrorize the settlements of western New York. This area was also the domain of the Iroquois League, an alliance of six warlike tribes. During the Revolution, four of these tribes—Mohawk, Seneca, Cayuga, Onandaga—joined the British.

The key to the Mohawk was Fort Stanwix, where Rome, New York, now stands. The fort was held by 750 Continentals under Colonel Peter Gansevoort and Lieutenant Colonel Marinus Willett, both able officers. Everyone in their command knew the history of the Bloody Mohawk, knew about people massacred after surrendering to enemies with large Indian forces. White commanders simply couldn't control the braves once they had defenseless captives in their power. And more than half of St. Leger's army were Indians. When a siege by St. Leger's troops began on October 3, the Fort Stanwix garrison vowed to fight to the end rather than surrender.

In the meantime, General Nicholas Herkimer of the New

York militia was coming with eight hundred reinforcements and tons of supplies. Herkimer's men, however, were poorly disciplined. Instead of keeping a sharp lookout, they talked loudly, straggled, and broke ranks whenever they felt like drinking from a stream. No one noticed eyes peering from the underbrush or painted figures darting among the forest shadows.

On August 6, six miles from Fort Stanwix, Herkimer's column entered a deep, narrow ravine near a place called Oriskany, "The Place of Nettles." The wooded slopes were studded with moss-covered boulders and old treetrunks. Indians and Tories hid there and in the brush just yards from the trail. Quietly, without moving a muscle, they waited for the perfect moment to spring their trap. Except for the marchers, the only sound was the caw and twitter of birds and the scurrying of small animals.

"*Sa-sa-kwon! Sa-sa-kwon!*" cried a chief, and the woods exploded.

Hundreds of Americans fell during the first seconds of firing, including their general. Herkimer took a bullet in the knee the same instant his horse was shot, throwing him from the saddle as it fell. When his head cleared, he had the saddle taken off his horse and placed in the shade of a tall elm. Mounted on it, he lit his pipe, drew his sword, and directed his battle. The attackers soon found that they had a tiger by the tail. Although badly hurt and cornered, the Americans fought back with desperate courage.

At first, Indians would wait for a man to fire his gun, then charge while he reloaded, crushing his skull with a tomahawk or a war club, a wooden club with a fist-sized stone tied at the end. Herkimer saw this and ordered his men to fight in pairs. As one man reloaded, his partner stood ready to shoot anyone who rushed forward.

The battle raged for two hours, until a thunderstorm burst. Since rain ruined gunpowder, everyone had to stop shooting until the storm passed. To the whites, the rain and lightning and thunder were an opportunity to rest and tend

*Although shot in the leg, General Nicholas Herkimer was able to direct the Battle of Oriskany from a sitting position.*

the wounded. To the Indians, they were signs that the Great Spirit was angry with his red children.

"*Oooo-nah! Oooo-nah! Oooo-nah!*" The cry of retreat echoed through the forest. The Battle of Oriskany ended as suddenly as it began, with not an Indian to be seen anywhere.

Herkimer's men were too tired and too few to go on. They gathered up their wounded and plodded away from Oriskany, leaving their dead unburied. American losses were 200 killed, 250 wounded and 200 captured, compared to 150 enemy casualties. Surgeons cut off Herkimer's leg, but he died with his Bible in his hand and his pipe clenched between his teeth. The siege of Fort Stanwix continued.

Things were looking pretty bad when General Schuyler asked Benedict Arnold to lead a 950-man relief column to the fort. Arnold knew his force was too weak to meet St. Leger in open battle. Very well; if he couldn't shoot his way to victory, he'd win through trickery.

A Tory prisoner named Hon Yost Schuyler had been sentenced to death for aiding the British. Now, this fellow was insane, which made him exactly the person Arnold needed for his trick. Arnold understood that Indians respected the mentally ill and sufferers from epilepsy, a disease that causes convulsions and strange visions. Such people were not thought of as being sick, but as "possessed" by spirits who told the future through them. Hon Yost was given an offer he couldn't refuse: his life for a lie. He accepted.

On August 22, Hon Yost ran into St. Leger's camp breathless and wild-eyed, his coat torn and shot through with bullet holes. He'd just escaped from the Americans, he said, and Arnold was coming with more soldiers than "the leaves on the trees." The Indians promptly ran away, forcing St. Leger to end the siege.

On the trail back to Lake Ontario, the Indians attacked their allies. British stragglers were tomahawked, their bodies stripped, and their packs stolen. It seemed only right, to the braves, that they should have some reward for all their trouble. Arnold entered Fort Stanwix with flags flying and bands playing the next day.

Burgoyne, ignoring his losses at Bennington and Stanwix, crossed the Hudson at Saratoga on a bridge of floating logs. Moving south ten miles, he found the way blocked by General Horatio Gates, Schuyler's replacement as army commander in New York. A retired British officer who'd settled in Virginia, Gates was nicknamed Granny, because of his white hair and wire-rimmed spectacles. Although he looked like a fussy grandfather, Gates knew how to run an army.

To reach Albany, Burgoyne had to get past Bemis Heights, overlooking the only trail along the Hudson's west bank. There, Thaddeus Kosciuszko, Gates's chief engineer, had built a line of trenches and breastworks. The only way around these defenses was through the thickly wooded hills farther to the west. But without Indians scouts, Gentleman Johnny couldn't find his way or get a picture of the American positions. He was, in effect, blind.

The armies clashed on September 19, 1777, at Freeman's Farm, a large wheatfield to the left of Bemis Heights. Gates wanted to lie low in his entrenchments and fight another Bunker Hill. Benedict Arnold, his second in command, disagreed; he insisted on protecting the left flank by going after the enemy. After an angry debate, Gates gave in, sending Arnold forward with the rifle companies and the infantry.

The British advanced in three columns, two of Redcoats and one of Hessians under Baron von Riedesel. The Redcoats approached behind a hedge of bayonets. Flags waved. Drummers set the pace. Bands played "The Grenadiers' March," a cheerful tune. Behind the infantry, artillerymen waited for the chance to open fire. Few lived to get that chance.

The Redcoats couldn't see Dan Morgan's riflemen hidden in the underbrush or high in the treetops. Suddenly Morgan gave the signal, blowing a turkey hunter's lure.

*Gobblegobblegobblegobble.*

His tooting was drowned by the crash of hundreds of rifles going off at once. Marksmen took special aim at British officers, a most "ungentlemanly" way of fighting. Artillerymen lay in heaps around their silent guns.

Gentleman Johnny made mistakes, but no one could call him a coward. He rode with his troops, shouting encouragement as bullets tore through his coat. Still, after three hours of fighting, the Americans were winning. Had von Riedesel not arrived in time, he might have been forced to surrender then and there.

The Redcoats fought bravely, as usual, but gained nothing. Over six hundred of them lay dead, including scores of boy lieutenants, the oldest of whom was seventeen. Lieutenant Hervey, sixteen and the nephew of a general, died pain-

LE GENERAL GATES CHEF
de l'Armée Américaine, qui fit capituler le
General Burgoine au Camp de Saharatoga le 16 8bre 1777.

*A French portrait of General Horatio Gates, the victor of Saratoga. Before joining the Continental Army, Gates had served for many years in the British army.*

fully. Courageous to the end, his last words were: "Tell my uncle I died like a soldier."

Burgoyne now dug in, in the hope that help would reach him in time. Although Sir Henry Clinton had led a small expedition up the Hudson to burn Esopus (modern Kingston), he had returned to New York City when American resistance stiffened. Gentleman Johnny was on his own.

On October 7, Burgoyne struck again near Freeman's Farm. By now, though, the Americans had the advantage in men and weapons. Gates's army numbered fifteen thousand, mostly militia, with newcomers arriving daily. Armed with French cannon and bayonets, they felt confident of victory.

The Redcoats were marching across the wheatfield when a chilling sound came from the edge of the forest: *gobblegobblegobblegobble*. Dan Morgan began the battle, but Benedict Arnold finished it. He'd recently resigned his command after a quarrel with Gates, but gunfire was music to his ears. Without orders, he leaped on a horse and galloped onto the field.

Arnold tore ahead, gathering troops as he went. He was a natural leader, and men followed him gladly and without question. Driven back near the enemy trenches, he rallied the troops for yet another charge. The Hessians broke. British General Simon Fraser was shot from the saddle. Arnold fell moments later with a bullet in the same knee that had been lamed at Quebec two years before. But he'd turned the tide. The British were so badly mauled that they dared not continue.

Soldiers carried Arnold away on a stretcher as he waved his hat to the thousands of cheering onlookers. None who saw him that day forgot his courage. Years later, when his name stood for "traitor," oldtimers still gave him his due. "A bloody fellow he was," said one. "He didn't care for nothing; he'd ride right in. It was 'Come on, boys!' 'Twasn't 'Go, boys!' There wasn't any waste timber on him. He was a stern-looking man but kind to his soldiers."

*A wounded Benedict Arnold turns the tide of battle at Freeman's Farm.*

The second battle of Freeman's Farm cost the British another 600 lives, the Americans about 150. Burgoyne was all but finished. When night came, he retreated to Saratoga. Gates surrounded him two days later.

The British situation went from bad, to worse, to hopeless. Food and ammunition were nearly gone. Sentries were found with throats cut and scraps of paper pinned to their bodies. The messages read: "For Jane McCrea."

The bombardment was awful. American guns boomed steadily, day and night, preventing sleep. Frederike, Baroness von Riedesel, took shelter with some officers' wives in the cellar of a ruined house. "My children," she wrote in her diary, "laid down on the earth with their heads upon my lap, and in this manner we passed the entire night. A horrible stench [from dead horses and oxen], and the cries of the children . . . prevented me from closing my eyes."

Burgoyne surrendered on October 17, 1777. As his troops handed over their weapons, an American band struck up "Yankee Doodle" and kept playing it throughout the ceremony. Redcoats no longer laughed at this tune.

News of Saratoga spread quickly. Englishmen were downhearted, for never in its long history had Great Britain lost an entire army. A London newspaper opposed to the war printed a none-too-funny poem:

> *In seventeen-hundred-and-seventy-seven*
> *General Burgoyne set out for Heaven;*
> *But as the Yankees would rebel,*
> *He missed the route and went to—Hell.*

Outside Philadelphia, George Washington's eyes grew watery and his voice broke as he gave his staff the news. Regaining his composure, he ordered a day of prayer and cannon salutes.

Happy as he was, the commander in chief couldn't have known, as we do, that Saratoga was the Revolution's turning point. Saratoga proved to King Louis XVI that the United States could, with help, win. Early in February 1778, he approved a Treaty of Alliance pledging France to fight alongside the infant nation. Spain joined the Allies in April of the following year.

GEORGE WASHINGTON'S worst battle during the winter of 1777–1778 wasn't with Sir William Howe, but with hunger, cold, and dirt. The British were living comfortably in Philadelphia when Washington sent the army into winter quarters. It marched to a bend in the Schuylkill River eighteen miles northwest of Philadelphia, near enough to keep an eye on

*Hard times at Valley Forge. Soldiers warm their hands over a fire, while comrades haul bundles of firewood.*

the enemy yet far enough to avoid being surprised by him. On December 17, it arrived at a village of a dozen houses built near an old ironworks. Valley Forge.

The troops found no camp, but a barren campsite ankle-deep in mud. With winter closing in, they had to work quickly. During the following weeks they built a thousand log cabins in a double line two miles long. Each cabin was sixteen feet long by fourteen wide with a stone fireplace, earthen floor, and roof of straw and branches. There were no windows.

Life in these cabins was nasty. When it rained, roofs leaked, turning floors into pools of stagnant mud. When the temperature dropped, the green wood being burned in the fireplaces filled the cabins with blinding smoke and made men cough as if their lungs would burst.

Bad as they were, the cabins might have been bearable with proper food and clothing. But Washington's troops had neither. There was never enough to eat. Doctor Albigence

Waldo, First Connecticut Infantry, kept a diary during his time at Valley Forge. It isn't pleasant reading, for there was nothing pleasant about life there. "It snows. I'm sick. Eat nothing. No whiskey. No forage. Lord, Lord, Lord . . . cold and uncomfortable. I am sick, discontented, and out of humor. Poor food. Hard lodging. Cold weather. Fatigue. Nasty clothes. Nasty cookery. Vomit half my time. Smoked out of my senses. The Devil's in it. I can't endure it. Why are we sent here to starve and freeze? What sweet felicities I have left at home, a charming wife, pretty children, good beds, good food, good cookery. . . . Here all confusion, smoke and cold, hunger and filthiness. A pox on my bad luck."

The cry of "No meat! No meat!" would begin at one end of camp and spread until it became a steady chorus. Day after day, men got along on firecake (a thin paste of flour and water baked on a hot stone) and water. Those lucky enough to have whiskey made "salamanders." They filled their tin cups with the raw alcohol, set it on fire, and swallowed it flames and all. Salamanders weren't very nourishing, but they kept off the chill for at least a little while. An officer found men in one cabin boiling a stone. "They say there's strength in a stone, if you can get it out," someone explained, smiling. Even at Valley Forge there was room for a joke.

Nakedness usually went along with hunger. What clothing there was had become little more than threadbare rags that gave no protection against winter's winds. The rule was share and share alike. When your turn came for guard duty, your cabin mates lent you their clothing. Even so, sentries were seen standing in their hats to keep their rag-wrapped feet out of the snow. Foreign visitors were amazed to see officers standing guard wrapped in old dressing gowns and shreds of blankets. Colonel Allen McLane poured whiskey into his boots to keep his feet from freezing. Lucky fellow: He had boots and whiskey to spare.

At least twenty-five hundred men died of disease at Valley Forge, more than Washington lost to enemy action during the entire Pennsylvania campaign. Weakened by hunger and cold, they fell victim to a long list of diseases: smallpox, typhus, influenza, pneumonia, scurvy. Lack of soap meant being dirty all the time. Dirt brought skin rashes, lice, and infection. Men were covered with chilblains, purple sores caused by long exposure to cold and damp. Frostbitten toes and feet turned white, then black, and had to be amputated to save the patient's life—maybe. Everything stank of dirt and damp and rot, which made General Anthony Wayne prefer a battle to making a camp inspection.

Sadly, much of this misery was unnecessary. There were plenty of supplies in Pennsylvania; the problem was getting people to sell them at fair prices. Farmers and tradesmen kept goods off the market to force up prices. Not that high prices guaranteed good quality. Americans sold their own army spoiled meat, wormy flour, and clothing that fell apart after a few days' wear. There were even those who traded with the enemy in Philadelphia.

Washington dealt harshly with such people. Many a farmer lost his goods and received 250 lashes for selling to the British. Foraging parties went in search of hidden supplies, which they took or paid for with "Continentals," near-worthless paper money issued by Congress. But men still died at Valley Forge.

Staying at Valley Forge could be harder on a man's spirit than on his body. Hundreds deserted not because of the miserable conditions, but because of letters from home. The Revolution often took a toll on soldiers' families as well. In small villages and isolated farms, men could not be spared for months or years at a time. There were shops to run, fields to plow, and crops to plant and harvest. Without a man to do the heavy work, wives and children might not survive. Officers reported soldiers coming to them, sobbing, with letters about how bad things were at home. Even loyal patriots deserted rather than have their families starve.

There were families, however, who believed so strongly in what their menfolk were doing that they kept their troubles

*Valley Forge, outdoor classroom. The Prussian Baron von Steuben taught the Continentals the basics of marching in formation and military drill.*

to themselves. Wives ran businesses, took in sewing, rented rooms to boarders—anything to make a few extra dollars. Children pitched in with the chores. They, too, became used to short meals and backbreaking work. Years later, an old man told how his mother always wrote his father cheerful letters, since "she would not weaken his hands, or sadden his heart, for she said a soldier's life was harder than all. . . ." Such women were the silent heroines of the American Revolution.

Valley Forge was not only a winter encampment but

an open-air school. In February 1778, as the Treaty of Alliance was being signed in Paris, a balding, red-faced man of forty-eight appeared at Washington's headquarters. He called himself Frederick William Augustus Henry Ferdinand, Baron von Steuben, lieutenant general in the army of King Frederick the Great of Prussia. Actually, he wasn't a nobleman; his highest rank was captain, and he'd not held a command for fourteen years. But he was an excellent drillmaster—exactly the man Washington needed.

Military drill was not just fancy marching in parades. Turning, about-facing, and quick-stepping in columns were essential battlefield maneuvers. The ability, for example, of thousands of troops to about-face as one man might make the difference between stopping an attack from behind and defeat, as on Long Island and the Brandywine.

Von Steuben turned brave fighters into disciplined soldiers. That wasn't easy, for Americans wouldn't obey orders blindly. In Europe, he wrote, "You say to your soldier, 'Do this,' and he doeth it. But [in America] I am obliged to say, 'This is the reason you ought to do that,' and he does it." If a lesson went well, he'd grin and grunt, "*Ach, gut! Sehr gut!*" If not, he'd let go with a mixture of German, French, and English curse words that made the troops double up with laughter. But they listened to him, and they learned. By the spring of 1778, they could march and use the bayonet like professionals. Men who'd been terrified of British steel were now eager to test themselves against it.

WHILE THE CONTINENTALS suffered and learned at Valley Forge, Sir William Howe decided that he'd seen enough of fighting in America and resigned his command. That was a wise decision for him personally, for Sir Henry Clinton, who took his place, was about to face a different kind of war.

In the spring of 1778, a French fleet sailed for the New World. British war planners weren't sure where they'd land, but they knew they could be used against the British West Indies, or to blockade New York, or to close the Delaware and pin Clinton between them and Washington's army.

To prevent these disasters, George III personally wrote Clinton's orders. The general was to evacuate Philadelphia while there was still time and concentrate his army in New York. He must also send ships and troops to reinforce the West Indies.

Clinton obeyed. Early in June, he sent three thousand Philadelphia Tories, two Hessian regiments, and most of the army's women to New York by sea. On June 18, he led the army, twelve thousand troops and a wagon train twelve miles long, out of Philadelphia. The plan was to march eastward

*Sir Henry Clinton became the last commander in chief of British forces in America during the Revolution.*

along a narrow road by way of Monmouth Court House, New Jersey, to Sandy Hook, where ships waited to carry them the last few miles to Manhattan.

As soon as Washington heard that the British were moving, he broke up the Valley Forge encampment and went after them. Here was a risk worth taking. If he could catch the enemy's main army strung out on the road, he might win a victory greater than Gates's, maybe even finish the war.

In the days that followed, the Continentals returned to places filled with painful memories. Private Joseph Plumb Martin found the country around Princeton a wasteland. The retreating British had destroyed whatever they couldn't carry away. Cattle were shot and left to rot in pastures. Wells were filled with garbage, houses burned, farm tools smashed. Redcoats even chopped down trees to get at the fruit. Frugal farmers winced at such senseless destruction, imagining their own farms after an enemy visit.

The Americans caught up with their prey a little beyond Monmouth Court House on the morning of June 28. Washington immediately sent General Charles Lee ahead with a strike force to slow the British until he arrived with the main army. Lee, a strange man who preferred talking to dogs rather than humans, was an experienced officer who'd served in the British and Polish armies.

Lee's experience didn't help him this morning. As soon as he attacked the British rear guard, Clinton turned and counterattacked with his whole army. Lee panicked. Instead of trying to hold on until Washington arrived, he ordered a retreat. The American front collapsed.

Washington knew nothing of this until he met soldiers rushing to the rear. Then he met Lee doing the same. Those who saw him gallop up to Lee never forgot the scene. He cursed Lee as a coward, took away his command, and sent him to the rear as unfit to be near brave men. Lee was later dismissed from the army, spending his last years alone, talking to his dogs.

Washington drew his sword and headed for the front. Bullets popped overhead. He ignored them. Cannonballs tore the ground before him. He kept going. "I have never beheld so superb a man," wrote Lafayette years later.

It was like magic. The sight of the big man on the big horse calmed the troops. Everywhere men stopped running.

Then, as von Steuben had taught them, they about-faced, straightened the line, and waited for the enemy with fixed bayonets.

Redcoats and Hessians charged, only to be flung back by massed volleys. These men were punished doubly. Yankee bullets were bad enough, but the heat was torture. June 28 was a muggy day with temperatures near one hundred degrees. Clinton's troops, clad in thick wool and carrying heavy packs, couldn't cope with the heat and fight at the same time. Whole squads toppled over and lay on the ground panting. Men died of sunstroke. Some poor fellows went insane; Clinton himself said he was "near going raving mad with heat." The Americans did better, for most were still in torn rags, which gave some relief. Even so, Private Martin called the battlefield "a heated oven."

The battle dragged on hour after hour. During the lulls between charges, the artillery dueled, making the soldiers more miserable—if that was possible. Among the American gunners was John Hays, a barber by profession. His wife Mary, or Molly, had been with him during his entire enlistment. This wasn't unusual; the Continental Army, like the British and Hessian forces, was always accompanied by hundreds of women.

Molly Hays, twenty-four, was a big woman who smoked, chewed tobacco, and used most unladylike language. The troops knew her and treated her as an equal. At least one man owed her his life; she found him left for dead after a battle and nursed him back to health. Another time, she asked a passing soldier to help her carry a pail of boiling water. He obliged so quickly that she asked his name. "George Washington," said he, bowing his head.

At Monmouth, Molly brought her husband's battery crew water from a nearby stream. She carried it in a pitcher, and made so many trips that the thirsty men began calling her Molly Pitcher.

Returning from one trip, Molly Pitcher noticed that her husband's gun was silent. John lay unconscious, the other crewmen dead. She dragged him into the shade and went back to the gun, loading and firing it singlehandedly until a relief crew arrived. She later received a pension for "service during the Revolutionary War" and died at the age of seventy-eight.

By late afternoon, both armies were exhausted. Fighting sputtered out as each waited for the cool of night. After making his final inspection, Washington wandered among some apple trees. Under one he found a youngster asleep on the bare ground without a blanket. Quietly the commander in chief lay down beside him, spreading his cloak over himself and the Marquis de Lafayette. Sir Henry Clinton rested his troops a while, then continued his march toward Sandy Hook and safety.

*"Molly Pitcher," heroine of the Battle of Monmouth, took over a cannon, loading and firing it by herself after its crew had been killed.*

The Battle of Monmouth Court House was a second turning point in the Revolution. Before Monmouth, every British commander dreamed of destroying the Continental Army in one glorious battle. Monmouth showed that this was impossible, that the Continentals were the regulars' equals in every way. It was the last big battle in the north. From then on, the British didn't dare challenge Washington to an all-or-nothing fight. Their main army kept behind its defenses in New York and the action moved to other fronts.

## · FIVE ·

# Yankee Doodle at Sea

$\mathcal{E}$ARLY in May 1775, at the beginning of the war, His Majesty's Ship *Falcon*, carrying eighteen guns, captured two American merchantmen off Cape Cod, Massachusetts. The people of New Bedford were so outraged that thirty husky lads piled into two small boats and chased after the "royal pirates." Overtaking them, they recaptured the merchantmen and threw *Falcon*'s crew into jail.

This incident, coming so soon after Lexington and Concord, opened another front in the American Revolution. The Revolution at sea was a big war fought on a small scale. It involved thousands of vessels and tens of thousands of seamen, although not all at once or in the same place. Instead of huge fleet actions, there were countless small fights, usually between no more than one or two vessels on each side. Yet those fights were as bitter and bloody as any on land, for they involved the highest stakes.

Control of the sea meant control of the land. The Royal Navy, George Washington said, was the British army's "canvas wings," enabling it to move faster, farther, and more secretly than on land. As long as the army held a seaport open to the navy, it could never be trapped.

This advantage, however, might also be a weakness. Every bullet, every uniform, every soldier needed in America had to come three thousand miles across the Atlantic Ocean. That voyage was never easy. If the winds cooperated, the east-west crossing took eighteen days; otherwise, it might take as long as three months. We know of ships that neared the coast and were then blown back and forth across the ocean several times. Thus the British lifeline was very long and very fragile. Cut it and the Redcoats, brave as they were, were doomed. Likewise, the Continental Army couldn't survive unless the sea-lanes to Europe remained open.

As a island people, the British had a thousand-year tradition of seamanship. Having defeated every European naval power—Spain, Holland, France—they thought of victory at sea as a natural part of their birthright. Yankee sailors would teach them differently.

When the American Revolution began, the Royal Navy had 270 warships, increasing to 468 by its end. Fighting ships in the 1700s were of three types. First came the ship of the line, ancestor of the modern battleship. A floating castle, the ship of the line weighed upward of two thousand tons and carried sixty-four to one hundred cannon mounted on two or three gun decks. Although slow and clumsy, nothing could stand up to it except vessels of its own class. In 1775 nearly half the Royal Navy's strength—131 vessels—was in ships of the line.

Next came the frigate, a 1,500-tonner with thirty-two to forty-four guns on a single deck. No match for its big sisters, this tall-masted beauty could crowd on acres of canvas to catch nearly anything afloat, which made it an ideal scout and hunter of enemy merchantships. Finally, there was the sloop of war with sixteen to twenty-four guns. Depending upon the number of masts and types of sails, sloops might be known as brigs, brigantines, and schooners. Lightweights all, they were useful in patrolling shallow coastal waters and blockading harbors.

Warship crews ranged in size from nine hundred men in ships of the line to sixty in the smallest craft. Every crew, however, was divided into two sections: common seamen who handled the vessel and specialists who fought. The common seaman was called a "tar," because he used tar to waterproof his hat, trousers, and other clothing. Tars had to dress comfortably to do their jobs. A man couldn't wear tight clothes and heavy boots if he had to climb tall masts to lower or furl sails. Seamen went barefoot to get a better grip on slippery decks and ropes, which made feet tough as shoeleather.

Fighting men spent most of their time with the guns. Naval guns were larger than the army's field artillery, which had to be hauled by horses and men. A large fieldpiece threw a twelve-pound ball a half-mile. A large naval gun sent a twenty-four pounder a mile and a half. The heaviest guns, called "smashers," fired sixty-eight-pound balls a half-mile. The sides of a ship of the line or frigate, though two feet thick, splintered like matchsticks when hit by large-caliber shot. Sometimes a ball passed clear through the ship, falling into the water on the other side.

Each gun had its own five- to nine-man crew, depending on its size. The gun was master, the crew its servant. Countless hours went into cleaning and polishing its barrel; an improperly cleaned gun might misfire or, worse, explode when fired, showering the deck with chunks of red-hot iron. Gunners constantly practiced loading their weapons, since quick firing meant more damage to the enemy. At night, they slept above the guns in hammocks slung from the gun deck's ceiling.

Naval guns fired different kinds of shot for different purposes. As with the field artillery, solid shot and grape shot put holes in targets and sprayed a large area like a shotgun. Bar shot, a smaller version of weightlifters' dumbbells, cut down masts. Chain shot, two iron balls joined by a chain, whirred through the air to cut rope rigging; sails were held in place by ropes, and without them a ship couldn't be steered. Spider shot, several two-foot blades joined at the top, slashed sails so they couldn't hold wind. Canister was a thin-walled metal can that burst, filling the air with rusty old nails, screws, and bolts.

Warships traveling alone or in small squadrons flew enemy flags or no flags at all. The idea was to come as near a stranger as possible and, if he turned out to be a weaker enemy, attack quickly. Once an enemy was identified, the captain "showed his true colors." The national flag was run up and drummers "beat to quarters," calling the crew to battle stations. Everyone knew what to do and did it—fast. Sailors climbed the masts and, perched two hundred feet above the swaying deck, prepared to take in or let out sail on command. Below, surgeons cleared tables and set out instruments. Cooks put out their fires. Carpenters readied sheets of lead to patch holes. Gunners sprinkled decks with sand to make them less slippery when blood flowed; to prevent panic, decks and walls were painted red.

Battle tactics were simple. When enemy fleets met, the ships of the line formed a line of battle with each a few hundred feet behind the other. The object was to "cross the *T*"; that is, each line tried to get ahead of the other and pass it at right angles, allowing the faster fleet to bring more guns to bear on the enemy's lead vessels. The same tactic applied when smaller craft met one-on-one. Each captain tried to set his ship at a right angle to the enemy's bow or stern in order to "rake," fire down his full length. It was hard to miss something vital during a raking. Masts toppled. Steering cables snapped. Ropes and chains whipped about wildly. Huge wooden splinters buzz-sawed through the air, turning decks to bloody shambles. Gunners, stripped to the waist, turned black as burned gunpowder clung to their sweaty skin. The dead, or what was left of them, were heaved overboard, as were the badly wounded, whom no surgeon's skill could save.

Yet cannon seldom decided a sea fight. The nature of wood is to float, so that unless fire broke out or lucky shots hit below the waterline, ships could survive terrific punishment. The cannon's real task was to cripple the enemy in order to strike the main blow. Sooner or later, the ships were deliberately crashed into each other. Grappling irons, small barbed anchors with ropes attached, were thrown across, and catching on the enemy's deck rails, the ships were tied together. Now the marines sprang into action.

Every warship carried as many as one hundred marines, its "soldiers of the sea." Marines normally served as ships' police, keeping the sailors in line, and as guards for the supply rooms, especially the liquor stores. During battle, marines stood behind the gunners, ready to shoot anyone who left his post. Most marines, however, fought. Teams of marine riflemen manned the fighting tops, platforms high in the masts from which they picked off men on the enemy's decks. They also threw grenades and stink pots, earthen jugs filled with sulphur, rotten fish, and other things that gave off thick, nauseating smoke.

At the officers' cry of "Boarders away!" marines stormed aboard the enemy vessel. Now it was every man for himself in a wild no-holds-barred brawl. With pistols and muskets, swords, axes, and spears, men fought until the weaker side gave in. A ship surrendered when its senior officer—the captain, if he was still alive—"struck his colors," ordered the flag taken down.

If a captured vessel could be salvaged, it was towed to port, sold as a prize of war, and the money divided among the victorious officers and crew. Since prize money was distributed according to rank, the higher the rank the larger the share. An admiral or captain could make his fortune from one rich prize. Common seamen had to be satisfied with the leftovers. If not, well, that was too bad for them.

Britain's naval victories were bought at terrible human cost. Life for His Majesty's common seamen was nasty, brutal, and often short. For a few pennies a day, the sailor risked his life in loneliness far from home. Voyages could last two or three years, during which time he might never set foot on land. The ship became both his home and prison. Although officers had cabins, the seaman slept in a hammock in a dark, crowded, stuffy compartment that smelled of dampness and dirt. Few slept soundly or through the night. Creaking timbers and the thumping of pumps interrupted sleep. It was also hard to ignore the scurrying and scraping of the ship's rats.

Sailors' food was never enough, and what there was was unappetizing. The sailor, said one report, "hath a stomach which ostridge-like could well neare digest iron." And a good thing, too. Meat was preserved in barrels filled with salt. "Salt junk," men called it: "Junk" was sailor talk for old rope and meat that had been in the barrel for so many years that it became a mass of ropelike fibers. Ship's biscuit, or hardtack, was bread baked hard as stone. Each piece, if it stayed in the barrel too long, was a mini-zoo filled with hopping, wriggling creatures. A veteran described hardtack:

> It was so light that when you tapped it on the table
> it fell almost into dust and thereout numerous insects
> called weevils crawled; they were bitter to the taste
> and a sure indication that the biscuits had lost its
> nutritious particles; if instead of these weevils, large
> maggots with black heads made their appearance,
> then the biscuit was considered to be only in the
> first stage of decay; these maggots were fat and cold
> to the taste, but not bitter.

Drinking was no better than eating. Water kept in leaky barrels turned foul, especially in the tropics. One ship's log notes that water taken on at Havana, Cuba, "began to stink, and look yellow, making us stop our noses whilst we opened our mouths." No wonder men looked forward to their daily pint of grog, watered-down rum. If you saved your grog ration for a few days and drank it all at once you'd become "groggy," drunk enough to forget your misery for a little while. But God help you if you were caught!

His Majesty's ships were ruled by terror. While at sea, a captain held the power of life and death in his hands.

His word was law, and he could do practically anything without being held accountable. He punished ordinary offenses with the cat-o'-nine-tails laid on the bare back. For example, drunkenness and gambling brought sixty lashes. Some captains had their own little "games." One man named Parker put an officer's coat on a pole and whipped every sailor who didn't salute it. In fact, any officer could beat any seaman. Even the twelve-year-old midshipmen, officers in training, used canes on sailors old enough to be their grandfathers.

Serious offenses—mutiny, desertion, striking an officer, cowardice—were punished savagely. Hanging might be a blessing compared to a thousand lashes, which often killed, crippled, or drove men insane. Offenders could also be "dropped from the main yard." A yard is a crossbar on a mast that supports a sail. The offender was hoisted to the top of the highest yard with a rope around his waist, dropped into the sea, and pulled up again—and again. In "keel-hauling," the victim was dragged under the ship by a rope. Then, if still alive, he was hung by the heels to get out the water.

Life in the Royal Navy was so bad that deserters always outnumbered volunteers. Thus, ships' crews had to be filled by impressment, or "pressing," forcing men to serve against their will. Impressment took place at sea and on land. A warship's captain could stop a British merchantman on the high seas and take anyone to fill a vacancy in his crew. Ashore, convicts and Redcoats dreaded no punishment more than being sent to the navy. "Press gangs" roamed British ports, knocking men over the head and dragging them aboard their ships.

Court records show that impressment destroyed whole families. With the breadwinner gone, women might steal in order to feed themselves and their children. But under British law, the penalty for stealing even a handkerchief worth two shillings—twenty-five American cents—was death by hanging. And the penalty was carried out, in public, even on starving women. Occasionally, children as young as twelve were hung as well.

Press gangs were also active in colonial America. In New York City, Royal Navy kidnappers broke into private homes to pull men from bed as frightened wives and children begged for mercy. During the fifty years before the Revolution, there were countless fights between press gangs and Americans in seacoast towns.

WHEN THE WAR BEGAN, the lighter British warships, operating in small squadrons, set out to teach the rebels a lesson. Coastal towns from Maine to Virginia were raided in the same way pirates once raided towns on the Spanish Main. Ships slipped over the horizon and opened fire before dawn, while townspeople still slept. Falmouth (now Portland), Maine, was bombarded with red-hot cannonballs and destroyed. Often, raiding parties of marines and sailors landed to arrest rebels, loot, and burn. Among the towns to suffer in this way were Fairfield, Norwalk, and New Haven, Connecticut, New Bedford, Massachusetts, and Norfolk, Virginia.

Such tactics, however, backfired. Soon local Committees of Safety organized lookouts and beach patrols, as well as militia to resist invaders. Congress even considered ordering Benjamin Franklin, its chief representative in France, to hire men to burn London, starting with the royal palace, but gave up the scheme as uncivilized. More important, Congress created the Continental Navy on October 30, 1775, and the Marine Corps a week later.

The American services were as different from the British as day and night. An able-bodied seaman earned eight dollars a month, over twice the pay of a British tar. Although American ships were as uncomfortable as any, the food was better and more plentiful.

Best of all, the American sailor was treated as a free man. Impressment was abolished; if a captain couldn't sign on enough men, he didn't sail. John Adams, author of the navy's first set of regulations, ordered captains to punish men "heard to swear and blaspheme the name of God" by having them "wear a wooden collar or some other shameful badge of distinction." Keel-hauling and dropping from the main yard were forbidden. Whipping was limited to twelve lashes. No man could be executed for any crime without a court trial and the approval of the commander in chief of the navy.

The Continental Navy's first four ships—*Alfred, Columbus, Cabot, and Andrew Doria*—were merchantmen purchased from their owners and fitted with cannon. *Alfred,* the largest, carried twenty nine-pounders, pop-guns compared to the armament of a ship of the line. Congress also raised money for building thirteen frigates. Ships of the line were too expensive for the infant nation. It had no intention of challenging the Royal Navy in fleet actions, but hoped to cut the enemy's supply line to North America.

Benjamin Franklin played a key role in these plans. Franklin was not only a famous scientist and journalist, but a diplomat who knew how to win friends for his country. In 1777, a year before the Treaty of Alliance, he persuaded the French to look the other way while he waged war from their soil. As Congress's chief representative in France, Franklin had the authority to buy vessels, equip them as warships, and commission officers in the navy. He used his authority well and often.

Among those he commissioned was Gustavus Conyngham, an Irishman with a talent for mischief. Franklin bought him the *Revenge,* a sleek cutter swift as greased lightning. No vessel, a British spy reported, could catch *Revenge,* but she could catch anything with sails.

Sailing from his base at Dunkirk on the French coast, Conyngham swept the North Sea and English Channel. He took sixty vessels in one year, prizes so rich that they paid for the entire American diplomatic service in Europe for the rest of the war. Once, when *Revenge* was damaged in a storm, Conyngham hoisted enemy colors and put into an English port for repairs.

At last Conyngham was captured and so mistreated that it seemed he'd die. To save him, Congress held a British

*Benjamin Franklin was an experienced diplomat popular with the French. As America's chief representative to France, he bought and outfitted ships to prey on British trade.*

officer hostage in return. Today we call hostage-taking terrorism, but in the eighteenth-century it was a normal way of guaranteeing an enemy's good behavior. In any case, Conyngham escaped, but the hostage didn't.

Franklin also helped a Scotsman named John Paul Jones become America's first naval hero. The son of a gardener, he was born plain John Paul in 1747 and went to sea at the age of twelve. After several voyages in a merchantman, he had to find another job when his employer went bankrupt. He signed on a "blackbirder," a slave ship bound for the African coast. But the slave trade disgusted him and he quit after two voyages.

While sailing home in another vessel, the ship's captain and first mate died of fever. John, a skilled navigator, brought her in safely. Her owners were so grateful that they made the twenty-one-year-old a captain and gave him a ship of his own.

John Paul worked hard and he expected others to do so as well. If they didn't, he used the whip, for the law allowed British merchant captains to beat their men. During a voyage to Tobago in the West Indies, he had the ship's carpenter whipped so severely for laziness that he died. That would have ended the matter, had he been a Royal Navy captain. But as master of a civilian vessel, he was charged with murder and kept in jail until cleared.

Jones's next command brought him back to Tobago in 1773. A mutiny by the crew forced him to run the ringleader through with his sword. Afraid to stand trial for another killing, he fled to America, adding Jones to his name to hide his identity. While in Philadelphia, he made friends with two members of Congress, who helped him get a lieutenant's commission in the navy.

People who knew John Paul Jones described him as five feet five inches tall, thin, with light brown hair, blue eyes, pointy nose, and tight-pressed lips. "His voice is soft and still and small," said John Adams, "his eye has keenness and Wildness . . . in it." Wildness. Yes, there was a wildness about him, and a courage that would never let him admit defeat. He had a bad temper and itched for a chance to prove himself in battle.

Jones's chance came with his first independent command, the sloop *Providence,* in the summer of 1776. After a successful cruise to Bermuda, in which he took sixteen prizes, he was promoted to captain. On June 14, 1777, he received orders to go to France with the eighteen-gun sloop *Ranger.* That

*Captain John Paul Jones was the American Revolution's greatest naval hero. From a 1780 drawing by Jean-Michel Moreau.*

same day Congress passed a resolution: "RESOLVED, That the Flag of the thirteen United States be thirteen stripes, alternate red and white; that the union be thirteen stars white in a blue field, representing a new constellation." It was Jones who first raised the Stars and Stripes on an American man-of-war.

As soon as he arrived in France, he reported to Benjamin Franklin. From the start the two men, so different in so many ways, liked each other. Jones explained that he wanted to do more than capture British merchantmen. He wanted to attack an enemy seaport, burn any ships he found there, and kidnap a nobleman to be held hostage for the release of American prisoners. Franklin liked the plan and gave permission to go ahead.

*Ranger* left France early in April 1778 and sailed into the Irish Sea between Great Britain and Ireland. Before dawn on April 23, she anchored outside Whitehaven, a port near the English-Scottish border. Whitehaven was a juicy target, its harbor crowded with three hundred vessels: merchantmen, coal-carriers, fishing boats. Two small forts stood at the harbor entrance, their guns zeroed in on the approaches.

Quickly, quietly, Jones led two boatloads of sailors past the forts in the darkness. Landing, they made their way to the first fort. Nothing stirred. The garrison was fast asleep. Raiders hadn't visited England since 1667, when the Dutch burned coastal towns, and no one expected them this morning. Since no ladders could be found, the sailors formed a human ladder by mounting the shoulders of the tallest and strongest men. Jones led the way, entering through a gun port. The garrison was awakened, tied up, and the guns' firing mechanisms broken. The second fort was taken the same way minutes later. Not a shot had been fired. Whitehaven slept.

Suddenly Jones's plan fell apart. One of *Ranger*'s crew turned traitor. As the others ran to the harbor, he went through the town shouting and banging on doors. Soon hundreds of men, many with swords and clubs, were gathering at the waterfront.

They found John Paul Jones alone on a pier, pistol in hand. He stood silently, his eyes fixed on the crowd, daring it to come forward. Behind him, sailors set one ship ablaze and then scrambled into their boats. As flames leaped skyward, he rejoined them for the trip back to *Ranger*.

Yet the day's work had only just begun. Jones raised anchor and headed for St. Mary's Isle, a tiny finger of land jutting from the Scottish coast nearby. There stood the mansion of the Earl of Selkirk, his intended hostage. The earl was away, but Jones's men wanted to loot the house. He allowed them to take the family's silver if they left Lady Selkirk and her servants alone. Jones, a gallant man who didn't make war on women, later bought the silver from his crew and returned it with a letter of apology.

Leaving Scotland, Jones crossed the Irish Sea. Next day, he sighted HMS *Drake*, a twenty-gun sloop of war, near Belfast in Northern Ireland. Drummers beat to quarters as both vessels closed for action. When they were near enough for voices to carry, *Drake*'s captain put his speaking trumpet to his lips. "What ship is that?" he shouted. "The American Continental ship *Ranger*," Jones replied at the top of his voice.

As the words left his mouth, the sides of both vessels erupted in clouds of gray smoke pierced by orange flashes. *Ranger* picked up speed and began to cross the *T*. Sliding across *Drake*'s bow, she raked her from stem to stern. Chain and grape shot smashed into her rigging. Ropes snapped and sails hung in tatters. *Drake* spun out of control as musket balls killed her captain. "Stop! Stop! By God, we strike!" someone shouted as her colors were hauled down. A boarding party found four dead and nineteen wounded Englishmen; *Ranger* had three killed and five hurt. Jones locked *Drake*'s crew below and had some of his men sail her to France as a prize.

The damage to Britain had been slight: two vessels lost and some silverware stolen. But the damage to Britain's pride and sense of security was tremendous. By bringing the war to the enemy's door, Jones showed that Britain could be attacked at will. The British public demanded more protection, forcing the Royal Navy to keep ships in home waters that would otherwise have been used against American towns.

Jones had the shock of his life when he returned to

France. For political reasons, *Ranger* was given to another captain and he was told he must wait for another command. He was beached. For the next year he pleaded for a chance to get back into action. Finally, thanks to Benjamin Franklin, the French, who were now in the war, gave him a six-ship squadron.

Jones's flagship was an old merchantman converted into a forty-gun frigate and named in honor of his friend. Back home in Philadelphia, Benjamin Franklin had published *Poor Richard's Almanac*, a collection of useful facts and wise sayings. Jones called his ship *Le Bonhomme Richard—The Good Man Richard—*after *Poor Richard's* creator. Most of her main battery of eighteen-pounders were worn and possibly unsafe, but they were guns and he decided to take a chance with them. Her crew was a mixture of American, French, and Portuguese seamen. In her, Jones fought the most famous ship-to-ship battle in American history.

Jones's second-in-command was Pierre Landais, a French officer on loan to the Americans, who sailed in the thirty-four-gun frigate *Alliance*. Landais was jealous of Jones and hated him more than the enemy. The rest of the squadron consisted of smaller craft with light guns.

Jones's mission was to scout the British coasts, taking as many prizes and damaging as many seaports as possible. His squadron put to sea in mid-August 1779. With Ireland to starboard—on the right—it sailed north, snapping up prizes along the way.

News that Jones was loose again threw Scotland into a panic. Militia units turned out. People flocked to the churches to ask God's help. One elderly parson had a chair brought to the beach at high tide. As the water lapped at his feet, he begged God to turn the wind about "and blow the scoundrel out of our gate." His prayers seemed answered when a gale forced two of Jones's ships to return to France.

The squadron rounded Scotland and moved down England's east coast. On September 23 many sails appeared off Flamborough Head, a chalk cliff jutting into the North Sea.

Jones had hit the jackpot: forty-one vessels filled with supplies for the Royal Navy. They were escorted by the new fifty-gun frigate *Serapis* (pronounced Se-ray'pis), captain Richard Pearson, and the sloop *Countess of Scarborough*. But there was no taking the merchantmen without first defeating these vessels.

Even though the strangers flew British flags, the convoy changed course and scooted away as soon as they were sighted. Its escorts turned, opened their gunports, and came forward to investigate. *Bonhomme Richard*'s escorts, however, crowded on every inch of canvas and darted away. Although one later captured the *Countess of Scarborough,* Jones had to face *Serapis* alone.

The sea was calm, the sun setting, as the distance between the vessels closed. "What ship is that?" Pearson cried.

"Come a little closer and I will tell you," Jones answered.

"What are you laden with?" asked the British commander angrily.

"Round, grape, and double-headed shot," was the reply.

The moon rose at that moment, shining on *Bonhomme Richard*'s flagstaff. The British flag was gone. In its place Pearson saw a black mass rising to the masthead. Reaching the top, it fluttered out into a banner twenty-five feet long: the Stars and Stripes.

Instantly each vessel's guns became kicking, flame-spitting monsters. *Bonhomme Richard*'s main battery had fired once or twice when two of its worn eighteen-pounders showed how deadly they really were. They exploded, killing their crews and those of guns nearby. *Bonhomme Richard* shook as a geyser of smoke and flame, wood and metal, burst through her upper deck. The other gunners, trembling and wide-eyed at the destruction around them, refused to touch

OVERLEAF:

*The night battle between HMS* Serapis *and the* Bonhomme Richard *was the greatest ship-to-ship engagement of the American Revolution. From an engraving by Richard Paton.*

the remaining eighteen-pounders. Jones, his heaviest guns useless, had only the lighter pieces on the gun deck and three nine-pounders mounted topside. His only hope now was to grapple and board *Serapis.*

But Pearson wouldn't give him that opportunity. The Englishman realized that he had the upper hand. His ship was faster and handier than *Bonhomme Richard* and, since the explosion, had all the heavy guns.

Pearson used his advantages well. Whipping in close to *Bonhomme Richard,* he fired murderous salvos and then slid away without a scratch. Once he called across to ask if Jones wanted to strike his colors. A voice came through the smoke, rising above the roar of battle. John Paul Jones's cry of defiance has become a United States Navy motto: "I HAVE NOT YET BEGUN TO FIGHT!"

These were brave words, but meaningless unless the enemy made a mistake. And that's exactly what he did. Pearson had ordered his sailing master to cut in front of *Bonhomme Richard,* in order to rake her, when he saw that the ships were on a collision course. He shouted for the sailing master to stop the turn, but it was too late. There was a sickening crunch as *Serapis*'s bow slammed into *Bonhomme Richard*'s starboard side near her stern. Men were knocked down and tossed about like rag dolls. The ships clung together for a moment, then a breeze brought *Bonhomme Richard* around in a half-circle until they lay alongside each other bow to stern and stern to bow. As they came together again, their yards and rigging became tangled.

Here was the chance Jones needed. Grappling irons were thrown onto *Serapis* and pulled tight, locking the ships together for the rest of the battle. "Well done, my brave lads!" shouted Jones. "We've got her now!"

The ships lay side by side with cannon muzzles only inches from each other's hull. *Serapis*'s eighteen-pounders banged away at pointblank range. One by one *Bonhomme Richard*'s guns fell silent, leaving only the three nine-pounders topside. She was fast becoming a wreck. The holes in her side were large enough, recalled Midshipman Nathaniel Fanning, that you could drive a coach and six horses through many of them. It was found after the battle that only a few supports kept the upper deck from falling onto the gun deck below. Her hold began to fill with water.

Several men, feeling the ship beginning to sink beneath them, wanted to surrender. "Quarters! Quarters, for God's sake!" a gunner shouted. Jones became furious at hearing one of his own men begging to surrender. His face flushed and the veins stood out in his neck as he cried, "Shoot them! Kill them!" He pulled a pistol from his belt and threw it at the man's head, knocking him cold. After that, no one aboard *Bonhomme Richard* dared ask for quarter.

The human wreckage was most terrible. The walls of *Bonhomme Richard*'s gun deck were spattered with blood and brains. Its floor was covered with blood that seeped through the planking and ran down the ship's sides in long streaks. Nathaniel Fanning thought she resembled a slaughterhouse in some weird nightmare: "To see the dead lying in heaps— to hear the groans of the wounded and dying—the entrails of the dead scattered . . . around and the blood [reaching] . . . over one's shoes, was enough to move pity from the most hardened and callous breast."

*Bonhomme Richard*'s crew thought themselves lost; then *Alliance* loomed out of the darkness. Saved! Men cheered as Captain Landais drew near and fired a salvo—into them. Cheers turned to cries of shock and pain as cannonballs plunged through their ship. Perhaps it was an error. Perhaps Landais had mistaken them for the enemy, although *Serapis*'s sides were bright yellow and *Bonhomme Richard*'s jet black.

It was no error. Landais knew what he was doing and fired several more times before turning away to watch the battle from a safe distance. He admitted afterward that he'd hoped to sink *Bonhomme Richard* and then capture *Serapis*, taking credit for the victory himself. Landais was dismissed from the Allied services as a lunatic, although that couldn't bring back those he'd killed.

Meantime, the British were having troubles of their own. By grappling early in the battle, Jones gave himself a real advantage. *Serapis*'s guns might smash *Bonhomme Richard*'s hull, but they couldn't be trained on her masts, which carried her fighting tops. American and French marines quickly cleared *Serapis*'s own tops and began to pick off men on her upper deck. Bullets pinged around Captain Pearson, an easy target in his blue coat and cocked hat, but none hit him; he was probably spared on Jones's orders. He was lucky, for *Serapis*'s upper deck was cleared of everyone except the dead.

The Americans grew bolder. When the yards became entangled, they formed a narrow, swaying bridge over each ship's deck. Yankee topmen began inching their way across until they hung over *Serapis*'s upper deck. From this dizzying height, hanging on by knees and toes, they fired into *Serapis*'s open hatches. Seaman William Hamilton did better. He took a bucket of grenades onto a yard and began dropping them. One fell through *Serapis*'s main hatch, landing in a pile of ammunition on the gun deck. Twenty Englishmen were blown to pieces. Blinded men, their hair and clothing afire, leaped screaming into the sea. Others were deafened and stripped naked by the blast.

At 10:30 P.M., after three hours of nonstop fighting, Pearson struck his colors. A moment later *Serapis*'s main mast tottered and fell overboard. So ended one of the fiercest sea battles of the age of sail.

The "butcher's bill," as Jones called it, was high. Of *Bonhomme Richard*'s 304-man crew, 150 were killed or wounded; *Serapis* lost 117 out of a 302-man crew. *Bonhomme Richard*, however, was finished. After desperate efforts to save her, she rolled over and plunged to the bottom of the North Sea. Her crew returned to France with their prisoners aboard the battered *Serapis*.

John Paul Jones became the hero of the hour. Songs and poems were written in celebration of his victory. Yet *Bonhomme Richard* proved to be his last fighting command in the Continental Navy. He was promised another, better, warship, but something always prevented him from getting it. After the Revolution, he served as an admiral in the Russian navy until poor health forced him to retire. A lonely man who never married, he died in France in 1792 at the age of fifty-five. His body was placed in a lead coffin filled with alcohol to preserve it and buried in a Paris cemetery.

John Paul Jones's remains were returned to the United States in 1905. The vessels that greeted his return would have warmed his sailor's heart. They were not wooden ships of the line, but twenty-thousand-ton steel battleships with guns that threw one-ton shells twenty miles. Today his body rests in a tomb at the United States Naval Academy, Annapolis, Maryland. Carved above the tomb in golden letters is a short sentence: I HAVE NOT YET BEGUN TO FIGHT.

THE DEFEAT OF *Serapis* was the Continental Navy's last victory. By late 1779, British shipyards were working round the clock. Scores of brand-new vessels were launched each year until the end of the war. These vessels drove the Continental Navy from the seas. Of the navy's thirteen frigates, nearly all were captured or destroyed, the rest bottled up in port by blockading vessels.

Unfortunately for Great Britain, these successes triggered a different kind of war, one that cost her dearly and that she couldn't win. With the Continental Navy neutralized, another type of Yankee ship, the privateer, took to the seas. The privateer was a licensed thief who waged "private war." For centuries governments had issued "letters of marque and reprisal" allowing their citizens to seize enemy shipping in wartime. Anyone with the means could buy a ship, sign up a crew, and attack, knowing he'd be treated as a prisoner of war rather than hung as a pirate if captured. Congress issued 1,700 letters of marque and reprisal during the Revolution.

The Atlantic coast of the United States was ideal for privateering. Scores of rivers empty into the ocean there;

hundreds of bays and inlets are protected from storms and from curious eyes. From 1776 onward, hundreds of tiny ship-yards sprang up in these out-of-the-way places. Seaports like Boston, Philadelphia, and Baltimore also built privateersmen.

These vessels were unlike any that had ever roamed the seas. Imagine a one-hundred-foot toothpick with sails and you'll have an idea of the privateersman's basic design. Its clean, sweeping lines, tall masts tilted back to carry clouds of sail, and needle-pointed bow made it more like an armed racing yacht than a man-of-war. Everything was sacrificed to speed and ease of handling. Although its twenty-odd cannon, usually six- and nine-pounders, were no match for a warship's armament, they'd make any merchant skipper see reason.

Yankee-built privateers could chase the smallest craft into the shallowest coastal waters or sail circles around the swiftest frigate. Their names were as varied as their owners' imaginations. They had patriotic names: *George Washington, Hancock, General Putnam, Bennington, Bunker Hill, True American*. There were also animal names chosen because they represented bravery or menace: *Eagle, Greyhound, Wolf, Snake, Skunk*.

It was easier for an adventurer to man a privateer than for George Washington to find the troops he needed. Men signed aboard a privateer out of a mixture of anger, need, and greed. The British blockade had been too effective. By stopping American trade, it threw thousands of seamen out of work. Angry men with families to feed, they gladly put to sea aboard a privateer. Thus, wherever British ships sailed, they went in fear, for there was no telling when an American privateer might appear over the horizon or dart out from a rain squall.

"The people are becoming privateering crazy," wrote John Adams, and he was right. The money was better than a seaman could earn from a lifetime of regular work. If he was lucky, one voyage could bring a thousand dollars at a time when families lived comfortably on nine dollars a month.

An Invitation to all brave Seamen and Marines, who have an inclination to serve their Country and make their Fortunes.

## The grand Privateer Ship DEANE,

commanded by ELISHA HINMAN, Efq; and prov'd to be a very capital Sailor, will Sail on a Cruife againft the Enemies of the United States of America, by the 20th inftant. The DEANE mounts thirty Carriage Guns, and is excellently well calculated for Attacks, Defence and Purfute—This therefore is to invite all thofe Jolly Fellows, who love their Country, and want to make their Fortunes at one Stroke, to repair immediately to the Rendezvous at the Head of His Excellency Governor Hancock's Wharf, where they will be received with a hearty Welcome by a Number of Brave Fellows there affembled, and treated with that excellent Liquor call'd GROG which is allow'd by all rue Seamen, to be the LIQUOR OF LIFE.

*Advertisement for a crew to man the privateer* Deane *that appeared in a Boston newspaper. Notice that anyone who enlists will be treated to grog, "the LIQUOR OF LIFE."*

The *Rattlesnake* alone took over a million dollars in prizes on a single cruise. A privateer captain had only to blow a bugle or beat a drum in any seacoast town to get more men than he needed.

One daredevil became an ace of his profession and a legend among seamen. Joshua Barney was born in 1759 on a farm near Baltimore. As one of fourteen children, he had to leave home to support himself in his early teens. He went to sea and, like John Paul Jones, was made captain for bringing a ship safely home after its master died in a storm.

Barney had a personal grudge against the British. He was a lieutenant on the Continental sloop *Saratoga* when

*Captain Joshua Barney, 1759-1818, fought the British in two wars. During the Revolution, his ship,* Hyder Ally, *captured the much larger British vessel,* General Monk. *During the War of 1812, he led raids on British commerce and was wounded trying to prevent the enemy from capturing Washington, D.C.*

she was disabled in a storm and taken by an enemy ship of the line. Barney and his comrades were packed into a tiny, damp, airless compartment three feet high, which prevented them from standing or sitting. They received practically no food or water for fifty-three days; eleven men broke under these conditions and died, some of them insane.

Once ashore in England, Barney was sent to Old Mill Prison, an awful place in which many died. One day he struck up a conversation with a Redcoat guard. He found that the guard had served in America, where a patriot had saved his life. Now he wanted to return the favor. He gave Barney a British naval officer's uniform and, when the coast was clear, let him pass through the gate. Barney made his way to the home of an Englishman known to favor the American cause, who smuggled him across the English Channel to France.

Barney returned home to become captain of the privateer *Hyder Ally*. He fought many battles and took many prizes, but his most famous exploit was against the British sloop *General Monk*. Barney won with a simple trick. As the vessels drew near, he told his sailing master to do the opposite of his next order. Then he shouted so *General Monk*'s captain could hear: "Hard-a-port your helm!" The British vessel turned sharply to the left to keep up, but the Yankee helmsman swung sharply to the right. As the vessels collided, Barney raked *General Monk* and in a minute had *Hyder Ally* lashed to her side. For years afterward, sailors marveled at Barney's neat trick.

LIKE THEIR CAPTAIN, the crew of *Hyder Ally* had scores to settle with the enemy. Every privateersman knew what to expect if captured. Since the colonies were in rebellion, and rebellion was illegal, the British government didn't recognize American letters of marque and reprisal. Thus American privateers were not prisoners of war in British eyes, but pirates who couldn't be hung, for fear of reprisal. The next best thing, therefore, was to keep them under conditions in which many would die anyhow.

Captured privateersmen were sent to the "hulks." In England, whenever jails became overcrowded, old warships were anchored in a river or bay and converted into hulks, or floating dungeons. Their rigging and masts were removed, gunports sealed, small air holes cut in the sides, and bars placed over the hatches. They were worse than any prison ashore.

During the Revolution, thousands of privateersmen were imprisoned in hulks anchored in Wallabout Bay in New York's East River, the future site of the Brooklyn Navy Yard. The worst of these was HMS *Jersey,* nicknamed "Hell Afloat." The best way to learn about the *Jersey* is to see her through the eyes of Captain Thomas Dring, who stayed there for five months toward the end of the war and lived to tell the tale.

Dring was amazed when he saw his fellow prisoners for the first time:

> "The faces of many of them were covered with dirt and filth; their long hair and beards matted and foul; clothed in rags, and with scarcely a sufficient supply of these to cover their disgusting bodies. . . . The skins of many of them were discolored by continual washing in salt water . . . [and] it was impossible for them to wash their linen in any other manner than by laying it on the deck and stamping it with their feet, after it had been immersed in salt water— their bodies remaining naked during the operation."

Although *Jersey* held 1,100 prisoners, with more arriving daily, overcrowding was no problem, since the dying made room for the newcomers. Each morning a Redcoat sergeant bellowed through the bars, "Rebels, turn out your dead!" No fewer than five bodies were hoisted up each day.

Prisoners were allowed half the Royal Navy's ration, and that was food rejected as too spoiled even for His Majesty's seamen. Rats and other vermin swarmed through *Jersey,* spreading disease. From time to time smallpox epidemics

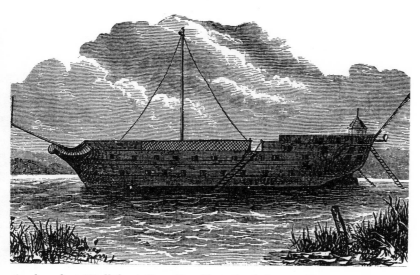

*Anchored at Wallabout Bay, Brooklyn, the infamous* Jersey *was a floating dungeon that took thousands of American lives.*

swept the hulk. A man might avoid this disease by innoculating himself in time. He'd "borrow pus"—take pus from the sores of someone recovering from the disease—and scratch it into the skin of his arm with a pin. This produced a mild infection, allowing his body's defense mechanisms to fight off a full-fledged attack later.

Prisoners gladly volunteered to bury the dead on the shore of Wallabout Bay. It was nasty work, but they were anxious to get ashore even for a little while. The feel of the earth between one's toes, the smell of fresh air, raised men's spirits and helped keep them alive. One of Captain Dring's friends once pulled up a clump of grass with the earth still clinging to the roots and hid it under his shirt. As soon as he returned, fellow prisoners divided the clump and passed it around like some precious gift. They held the grass and earth under their nostrils, inhaling the aroma of freedom.

There were two ways of escaping the horror of the hulks. One was to go over the side and swim the two-and-one-half miles to shore. But this was dangerous for sick, undernour-

*American privateers suffered greatly aboard the prison hulk* Jersey, *as we can see from this drawing by John Trumbull.*

ished men, and the guards were quick to shoot. Even if one reached shore, Long Island was Tory country, where people were eager to collect rewards for fugitives.

The other way was to enlist in the service of King George III. British officers constantly spoke of His Majesty's generosity toward rebels who mended their ways. Yet very few accepted the offer to turn traitor. Their willingness to suffer is proof of their devotion to the cause of American independence. Each Fourth of July they made little flags from old rags. At night, crowded in their foul quarters, they sang a song with the verse, "For America and her sons forever shall shine." The flags and singing infuriated the guards, who cut their rations for a few days afterward. Over eleven thousand privateersmen died in the hulks, more than George Washington lost in all his battles.

This was a heavy price to pay in lives and suffering, but the privateers hurt the enemy worse than the Continental Navy. Privateers took 3,087 British merchantmen, compared to 196 for the navy, which also took 102 enemy men-of-war. Such losses, while they couldn't bring the British Empire to its knees, certainly made people think about the wisdom of continuing the struggle.

## · *SIX* ·

# Frontier People

*I*N THE YEAR 1779, the vil-
lage of Minisink in western New York State had a one-room
schoolhouse. Mr. Jeremiah Van Auken, the schoolmaster,
was a busy man, for he had to teach different subjects to
children of different ages at the same time. On July 20, he
glanced out the window and saw a Mohawk war party coming
from the woods. Quickly he sent the children running home
to warn their parents. Then, to give them a head start, he
went to meet the Indians alone. "Brother!" he said, holding
out his hand to a painted brave. It was the last thing he
ever did. The brave killed Mr. Van Auken with one blow
of his tomahawk and scalped him. This was not the first
time, nor would it be the last, that Indians killed innocent
people in the name of His Majesty King George III.

The Indians and British were natural allies. After the
French and Indian War, settlers began crossing the Allegheny
Mountains into the fertile lands of the Ohio Valley. Land
for these people meant farms and homes and a chance to
better themselves through hard work. The Indians, however,
saw the newcomers as invaders come to steal lands that, they

believed, the Great Spirit had given them at the beginning of the world. Experience taught them that the White Eyes would do anything to get land. And once the White Eyes got it, they cut down the forest, slaughtered the game, and wounded the earth with their plows. Indians worshipped nature and saw this as an insult to their religion. Worse, they feared that they'd lose their way of life, becoming outcasts in their own land.

In 1763, Chief Pontiac of the Ottawas led the western tribes in a war to destroy the new settlements. He failed, but his war had been so costly that King George's government decided it couldn't afford another Indian uprising. The Proclamation Line of 1763 closed the lands west of the Alleghenies to white settlement. Families already in the area had to leave, abandoning farms and settlements carved from the wilderness with backbreaking work. Although the Proclamation Line pleased the Indians, it angered the colonists at the very time trouble began over the Stamp Act. Anyone who wanted to better himself in the west faced two enemies: the Indians and the British government.

The coming of the Revolution forced the Indians to take sides. If they remained neutral, as Congress hoped, the British would stop supplying the trade goods—muskets, gunpowder, iron knives and tomahawks—they needed but couldn't make for themselves. But if they joined the British, and the British won, settlers might be barred from their lands forever. Their choice was clear. By 1779, the warlike tribes of the Ohio Valley and the Iroquois League of New York smoked the war pipe with British agents.

The British planned to use the Indians in a war of extermination. General William Tryon, the last royal governor of New York, admitted that they wanted to "loose the savages against the miserable Rebels in order to impose a reign of terror on the frontiers." Its target was not the enemy military but civilians; its purpose was to cause so much misery that people would beg for peace at any price.

This war of extermination was launched from bases near

the Great Lakes. Fort Niagara south of Lake Ontario gave access to the waterways leading to western New York and Pennsylvania. Fort Detroit on Lake Erie menaced the Ohio Valley, the Illinois country, and Kentucky.

Warriors came to these bases for supplies, guns, and ammunition. Often they were joined by the dreaded Greens, Tory rangers dressed in green uniforms to blend with the forest. Tories, having been driven from their homes in the east, fled to the frontier to carry on the struggle. Bitter men haunted by bad memories, they could be as fierce as any Indian. The frontier people hated them. A Virginia judge named Lynch gave Tories a quick trial and a quicker hanging. His brand of justice gave the term "lynch law" to our language.

THE NEW YORK–PENNSYLVANIA frontier caught fire when the chief of the Mohawks joined the British. His Indian name was Thayendanegea—Bundle of Sticks—but whites knew him as Joseph Brant. He was a wise man and a great war leader.

Joseph Brant was born about 1742 and learned to live in both the Indian's and the white man's world. His early years were spent in the forest doing as other youngsters did: hunting, fishing, swimming, canoeing, and learning the ways of the warpath. At the age of nineteen he went to live with an English missionary and became a Christian. He learned so well that he helped translate the Bible into Mohawk. As the Revolution drew near, he was invited to London to make sure of the Mohawks' loyalty to Great Britain. Artists and poets, noblemen and Cabinet ministers, treated him as an honored guest. One day he'd stroll around town dressed as an English gentleman, the next in the outfit of a Mohawk chief.

Brant pledged his loyalty to the British and always kept his word. Returning to America in 1776, he rallied not only his Mohawks but most of the Iroquois League against the rebels. Sometimes he joined forces with Butler's Rangers. This group, led by John and Walter Butler, a father-and-

son team of wealthy Tory landowners who'd lost their property in New York State, was the most feared of all the green bands.

Once Brant took the warpath, he stayed on it for the entire Revolution. He fought bravely and skillfully, making the rebels pay a fearsome price. It was he who'd set the trap that nearly destroyed General Herkimer at Oriskany. But his and the Butler's real skill was hit-and-run raids against civilians.

The Indians were especially good at this type of fighting. Their method, developed during centuries of warfare among themselves, had three parts: attack without warning, kill swiftly, and escape before the enemy could gather his strength. Every raid followed this pattern; only the targets and the victims differed.

The typical raid was carried out by a war party of between twenty and forty braves. The rule was "smaller is better," for the smaller the group, the faster it could travel and the better its chances of avoiding detection. Sometimes, usually when joined by Tories, as many as two hundred braves took part in a raid. Larger war parties had the advantage of being able to fan out across the countryside, causing more damage.

The Indians' favorite targets were isolated farms and the village without a stockade, a small fort surrounded by a wall of logs set in the ground, with their tops sharpened to a point. The best time to attack was before dawn, when people were asleep.

The first sign of danger was noise. People were startled awake by gunshots, rattles, whistles, and war whoops. The noise, like everything a raiding party did, had either a religious or a practical purpose. Noise confused victims, spread panic, and paralyzed them with fear.

*Mohawk Chief Joseph Brant led his people in raids against settlements in frontier New York and Pennsylvania. From the painting by George Romney.*

*Tories and Indians massacred settlers in the Wyoming Valley of Pennsylvania leaving hundreds dead and a thousand homes destroyed.*

If the whites offered strong resistance, the braves broke off the attack and faded back into the forest. Indians felt no shame in running away and living to fight another day. Tribes were small and each life precious. Losing a warrior meant one less hunter to feed the tribe, one less protector in times of trouble. Indians couldn't afford last-ditch stands or fights to the finish. Although they valued courage, they knew it wasn't the same as taking needless risks.

If all went well, they pressed the attack without mercy. Within seconds, any guards or men who happened to be about were shot from cover. Painted braves then broke down cabin doors and crashed through windows, firing guns and swinging tomahawks.

Once in control, the Indians began the grisly task of scalping the dead. The custom of scalping was very ancient in North America. Indians believed that one's spirit or soul lived in the hair at the top of the head. Thus, taking the scalp captured the enemy's spirit and prevented his ghost from seeking revenge. Scalps were also proof of a brave's courage, like soldiers' medals. They were dried on small wooden hoops, painted with the brave's personal designs, and worn on belts or hung on poles in front of his wigwam. Braves would pass the long winter nights around the fire, bragging and describing how they took each scalp.

Meantime, the captives—if there were any—were lined up for selection. The wounded, old and infirm, as well as young children, were tomahawked and scalped; they couldn't keep up and might endanger the war party on its way home. Healthy men, women, and half-grown children were bound with leather "slave straps" and marched away.

But before leaving, the Indians stole whatever took their fancy. They were especially fond of women's clothes, and war parties often returned wearing colorful dresses, shawls, and bonnets. Then they destroyed everything they couldn't carry away. Farm animals were slaughtered. The farm was burned, together with the crops growing in the fields. The dead, as a final insult, were mutilated to strike terror into those who'd soon rush toward the rising smoke.

The prisoners' ordeal, however, had only just begun. When they reached the Indian village, they were forced to run the gauntlet; that is, run between a double line of villagers who hit them with clubs. Any who fell were killed and their bodies thrown to the dogs.

The surviving runners were brought before the tribal council to learn their fate. A few might be sold to the British or held until relatives sent ransom money. Some were adopted into the tribe. Any squaw who'd lost a relative could claim a captive to take his or her place. From the moment of adoption, captives were treated as if they'd been born into the tribe. Children were loved by their new parents as their own and raised as Indians. Adults might have Indian wives or husbands. In time, thousands of captives became "white Indians," often refusing to return to the white world, even when they had the chance. Adopted boys sometimes became war chiefs and fought against the whites.

Women not held for ransom or adoption became slaves in a warrior's family. Men were smeared with charcoal and tortured to death. Although this shocked whites, it was no more than Indians expected for themselves if taken by enemy tribesmen.

A victim was tortured slowly and in the most horrible ways. He was made to walk barefoot over live coals. Tomahawks heated red-hot were hung around his neck. Muskets filled with gunpowder but without bullets were fired into his body. His fingernails were pulled out, his ears and nose cut off, his belly opened, and his intestines wound around a stick. He was scalped and burning coals heaped on the open wound. Indian women and children, as well as warriors, took part in the torturing.

The Indians admired courage and the ability to withstand pain. By not crying out, the victim showed that he was better than his torturers. The bravest victims were honored by being eaten.

*Mohawk* is an Indian word for "man-eater," because that was exactly what this and other tribes did. The Eastern Woodland Indians were not cannibals—users of human flesh for food. Yet they did believe that a brave man's blood and body were full of magical power. By eating these, they hoped to add to their own courage; the heart especially was prized as a source of courage.

RAIDS OCCURRED almost daily. The years 1778 and 1779 were a sad time in frontier New York and Pennsylvania. In July 1778, Butler's Rangers devastated the Wyoming Valley of northeastern Pennsylvania. Joseph Brant joined Walter Butler later that year in raiding Cherry Valley, fifty miles west of Albany, New York. In July of the following year, Brant led Mohawks and braves from other Iroquois tribes against Minisink in the Mohawk Valley.

Joseph Brant spared women and children whenever possible during these raids, which made him unusual among Indian war chiefs and Tory rangers. In Cherry Valley, Butler's men broke into a house where a woman had just given birth and were about to tomahawk mother and child when Brant came by. "What," he shouted, "kill a woman and child! No, that child is not an enemy of the king, nor friend to Congress. Long before he is big enough to do any mischief, the dispute will be settled." He set a guard at the door and they were saved.

At Minisink, after schoolmaster Van Auken's murder,

braves caught up with some of the fleeing girls. Seeing this, Brant placed his paint mark on their dresses, which meant they were his personal property and not to be harmed. The girls made the paint marks go a long way by sitting beside their brothers and spreading their dresses over their laps.

Unfortunately, it wasn't always possible for Brant to help, since he couldn't be everywhere and braves easily got out of control. As a result, settlers were slaughtered and their villages left as heaps of smoking rubble. In the Wyoming Valley, the largest raid of the war, a thousand homes were burned, hundreds were killed, and scores tortured to death.

These attacks shocked not only Americans but Englishmen of conscience. Former prime minister William Pitt was ashamed of his country. Great Britain, he told Parliament, was fighting an "unconstitutional, illegal, and unchristian" war on the American frontier. "We turn loose these savage hell-hounds against our brethren and countrymen in America, of the same language, laws, liberty and religion, endeared to us by every tie that should sanctify humanity." Yet words alone, even from such a man, couldn't stop atrocities that the government thought necessary to fighting the war. Action—strong action—was needed to do that.

In the spring of 1779, Washington decided that he had to take action. He chose General John Sullivan of New Hampshire to break the Iroquois. He gave Sullivan, who'd served in every battle from Long Island to the Brandywine, the best he had: four thousand veteran Continentals, including Dan Morgan's riflemen, and a dozen field guns.

Sullivan's orders were to strike north from the Wyoming Valley into the Finger Lakes region of New York. There, in the Iroquois heartland, he must bring about "the total destruction and devastation of their settlements." The Iroquois were not only hunters and warriors, but skilled farmers who lived in villages with hundreds of people. By ruining their lands, Washington meant to give them a taste of their own medicine and force them to stop their raids.

Joseph Brant and the Butlers tried to ambush the invaders at Newtown near the New York border, where the city of Elmira now stands. This time, however, the ambushers were themselves ambushed. Sullivan's scouts noticed the trap and gave the alert. He sent riflemen through the woods to the enemy's rear while his artillerymen unlimbered their guns.

Indians and Tories were caught in a crossfire. As the riflemen banged away, shells burst overhead, setting brush fires and snapping trees like twigs. The Indians were terrified of the "wagon guns," whose fire and thunder seemed that of angry forest spirits. Despite Brant's encouragement, they ran away after only a few minutes' fighting. There were no more battles after Newtown. Except for an occasional skirmish, the Iroquois homeland lay open and defenseless.

Sullivan's army bulldozed its way through a Garden of Eden. Few colonists had visited the Finger Lakes area and the men were amazed at what they found. There was acre after acre of corn higher than a horse's head. Apple, pear, and peach trees were heavy with fruit. Fields overflowed with potatoes, pumpkins, squash, cucumber, watermelon, beans, and peas.

The Americans now had their turn at burning, looting, and taking souvenirs. Every village and field was torched. Orchards were cut down. Soldiers filled their pockets with beans and marched with melons spiked on their bayonets. Dead Indians were scalped and sometimes skinned. Lieutenant William Boyd wrote in his diary: "At the request of Major Piatt, sent out a party to look for some dead Indians. . . . Toward noon they found them and skinned two of them from their hips down for boot legs: one pair for the Major and the other for myself." Neither side had a monopoly on cruelty in this terrible border war.

Wyoming Valley captives—mostly women and children—were found in an abandoned village. They were in such bad shape, and told such horrible stories, that some soldiers forgot they were supposed to be civilized men. Finding an old squaw and a crippled boy in a cabin, they nailed the door shut and set the cabin on fire.

*The bleeding frontier. During the Revolution, Indians joined Tories, Americans loyal to King George III, in raiding frontier settlements. In reprisal, General Washington sent troops to burn Indian villages, as they are doing in this drawing.*

When there was nothing else to destroy, Sullivan returned to Pennsylvania. Left behind were the ashes of forty-one villages and 160,000 bushels of corn, which forced the British to support thousands of homeless Iroquois that winter. The Indians knew who'd given Sullivan his orders. To this day George Washington's Iroquois name is "Town Destroyer."

Yet Sullivan's expedition was a failure because he didn't destroy Fort Niagara. It was like cutting weeds without pulling up their roots. Before long, the Indian menace was stronger than ever.

The Iroquois swore revenge for that summer of 1779. The next two years were the worst in the history of the New York frontier. Brant and the Butlers rallied their forces at Fort Niagara and returned to the attack. Cherry Valley and Minisink were visited again with heavy loss of life. Prosperous settlements at Canajoharie and Caughnawaga on the Mohawk

River went up in smoke. Schoharie on the Schoharie River, a branch of the Mohawk, was destroyed. The Oneidas, a member tribe of the Iroquois League that sided with the Americans, were driven from their homes by Brant's warriors. Congress answered with further reprisals against Indians and Tories.

And so New York's frontier war continued, each side claiming an eye for an eye and a tooth for a tooth until it seemed that both would be blind and toothless. It ended in 1781, when the Revolution's military operations came to an end. But by then the settled area between the Mohawk and the west bank of the Hudson was a wasteland. Even proud Fort Stanwix had to be abandoned.

The only bright moment for the settlers came that year with news of Walter Butler's death. Settlers called him "Hell Hound" Butler because of his cruelties. He'd been shot off his horse and wounded by an Oneida scout. "Quarter! Quarter!" he cried as the scout ran up to him. The Oneida raised his tomahawk, shouted "Cherry Valley quarter!" and split his skull.

Although Brant and the elder Butler received lands in Canada after the war, the Iroquois were ruined. Their worst defeat was not on the battlefield but at the peace table, where they weren't represented. The peace treaty said nothing about Indian rights; indeed, Great Britain gave the United States all Indian lands east of the Mississippi River. Thus, the American Revolution was the beginning of the end for those who'd ruled the Eastern Woodlands since before Columbus landed in the New World.

THE FRONTIER WAR also raged in an area where there were no English settlers until the 1770s. The Northwest Territory was bounded by the Allegheny Mountains, the Mississippi and Ohio rivers, and the Great Lakes. This was a land of virgin forests, sparkling lakes, and broad prairies teeming with game. Here roamed the elk, the grizzly, and the wolf. Buffalo herds, which in colonial times ranged from the Great

Plains to the banks of the Mississippi, trampled "traces," trails several feet deep, to their feeding grounds and salt licks.

The Northwest Territory was home to the western tribes: Ottawas, Hurons, Delawares, Potawatomis, Kickapoos, Miamis, Illinois, Ojibwas, Cherokees, Shawnees. And beyond, where the sun slept at the end of each day, were the Sioux and Cheyennes, proud peoples whose struggle with the White Eyes wouldn't really begin until the first centennial of American independence.

The Indians shared tiny patches of their domain with whites who'd come down from Canada. For nearly a century, the French had three main settlements in the area. There was Kaskakia on the Mississippi in what is now the state of Illinois. Cahokia also lay on the Mississippi near modern East St. Louis, Missouri. Vincennes is on Indiana's Wabash River. The French, fur traders rather than farmers, got along well with the tribes; their young men often married squaws and were as comfortable in tipis as in log cabins.

When the French and Indian War ended, the British took over these settlements and Fort Detroit, France's main military base to the north. Although the settlers had to swear allegiance to King George III, the British left them to themselves. They controlled the valuable fur trade and lived peacefully with the tribes, which was all His Majesty's government expected of them.

Americans began crossing the Alleghenies in the year of Lexington and Concord, when Daniel Boone led the first settlers through Cumberland Gap into a place of breathtaking beauty. Indians called it *Ken-ta-ke,* "The Great Meadow." Kentucky abounded with game of every kind. Travelers told of hillsides blazing with azalea, and how their horses' legs became reddened from walking through fields of strawberries. The flow of air out of Mammoth Cave meant, to the Indians, that Kentucky was a spirit land, the place where the earth breathed. Indians also knew it as The Dark and Bloody Ground, for each tribe would kill to keep intruders from its hunting grounds.

The Indians saw Daniel Boone's settlement of Boones-borough on the Kentucky River as the edge of an axe biting into their territory. It had to go. Trouble began the moment the first logs were driven into the ground for the stockade and the first fields broken by the plow. Ambushes, scalpings, burning: It was the old pattern familiar in the East.

On July 14, 1776, as news of the Declaration of Independence flew across the land, Jemima Boone, fourteen, and two of her friends were kidnapped by Indians as they picked flowers along the bank of a stream. Their kidnappers were Shawnees, among them the son of the famous Chief Black Fish.

Jemima and her friends had been born and raised on the frontier. They learned from childhood that, whatever happened, they must master their fear and think clearly. They also knew that help would be on the way as soon as they were missed. Their job was to guide the rescuers by leaving a trail. Jemima, who was barefoot, ground her heels into the soft earth. Betsey Callaway and her sister, Fanny, made footprints with their shoes. When the braves weren't looking, they quietly snapped twigs and left tiny pieces of cloth from their dresses clinging to the brush. They were as cooperative as fox cubs.

For two nights and a day they traveled until the kidnappers, feeling safe, stopped for rest and a meal of broiled buffalo hump. That was a mistake, because Daniel Boone had easily read the girls' "signs." By stopping, the Indians allowed the rescue party to catch up. The girls were sitting with their backs to a tree, watching the Indians prepare the meal, when shots rang out. Black Fish's son pitched headlong into the fire; another brave clutched his chest as blood spurted from between his fingers.

"That's Daddy!" cried Jemima.

The coming of the Revolution meant bigger trouble for the Kentuckians. Lieutenant Governor Henry Hamilton, the British chief at Fort Detroit, received orders from London to start a full-scale Indian war. Hamilton followed his orders to the letter. Bands of warriors were invited to Detroit to receive gifts of guns and firewater. The governor promised a reward for each American scalp brought to Detroit; he didn't care whether it was a man's, a woman's, or a child's. "Hairbuyer Hamilton" became the most hated white man west of the Alleghenies.

Attacks on Boonesborough and settlements that had been built elsewhere increased. In February 1778, a Shawnee war party captured Boone himself at the Blue Licks, where salt deposits had been discovered. Its leader was Chief Black Fish.

The chief smiled as his men formed a double line. Calmly, Boone walked up to the line and said, in perfect Shawnee, how pleased he was to run the gauntlet against Black Fish's braves: "We will see which can hit hard and which hit like children." Suddenly he lowered his head and ran between the lines. Clubs and fists came down on him, but he swerved from side to side, either too close or too far for the blows to land with full force. When a brave stepped in front of him with a raised club, Boone, bending even lower, butted him in the stomach and sent him sprawling. The others shook with laughter and Boone reached the end of the gauntlet seconds later.

Black Fish smiled, for the Great Spirit had sent as a substitute for his son the very man who'd killed him. Big Turtle, as he'd be called from then on, was handed over to the village squaws before the adoption ceremony. They stripped him naked, dunked him in an icy creek, and scrubbed him until every trace of "whiteness" disappeared. They plucked out his hair, painted him with the tribal symbols, and dressed him as a warrior. That night Big Turtle smoked the pipe with his Shawnee brothers.

Big Turtle spent the winter doing what he liked best: riding, roaming the woods, hunting. But he also hid a supply of dried meat, gunpowder, and bullets. In the spring, Black Fish announced that the Shawnees were returning to the war path. Target: Boonesborough.

Big Turtle had learned to respect Black Fish and love

his Indian "mother," but he had his own family at Boonesborough. At the first opportunity, he escaped.

A farmer near Boonesborough saw an Indian limping out of the woods. He went for his rifle but something about the fellow seemed familiar. "By God!" he muttered. "Daniel Boone! By God!" At forty-three, Boone had come through 160 miles of wilderness in less than four days and had outwitted Indian trackers.

Boonesborough prepared to defend itself against the coming attack. Food and animals were brought in from the farms and the well was deepened. Everyone knew where to go and what to do during a siege. Men would fire their rifles through loopholes in the walls. Women and teenage boys would reload the rifles as quickly as possible. Younger boys and girls would stand by with water buckets to douse fire arrows. Hatchets, knives, clubs, and pitchforks were stockpiled in key places, for the people intended to sell their lives dearly if the Indians broke through the stockade. They'd never surrender.

Black Fish arrived with his braves at the beginning of September 1778. He wasn't angry, he said, about his "son's" escape, only disappointed. He still loved Big Turtle, he said, but the White Eyes and Shawnees were at war and must fight.

And fight they did. For eight days the Indians tried to break into Boonesborough. They tried to burn out the defenders. They tried shooting them off the walls. They tried tunneling under the walls. Nothing worked.

They tried taunting the people to lower their spirits. In reply, Squire Boone, Daniel's older brother, built a cannon out of a hollow log, packed it with gunpowder, and loaded it with rifle bullets. It mowed down several braves on the first shot. Too bad it exploded at the next one. Finally, when their tunnel collapsed during a cloudburst, the Indians decided to leave Boonesborough alone for the time being.

The war in Kentucky now became more desperate than any known in the East. When the settlers crossed the mountains, they had turned their backs on civilization. Unlike the people of western New York and Pennsylvania, who might have soldiers to protect them and could flee to the coastal cities, the Kentuckians were on their own.

Being alone wasn't easy. Here are typical diary entries for one week at Harrodsburg, Kentucky: "We had 4 Men wounded and some Cattle killed. . . . Indians killed & scalped Hugh Wilson. . . . Archibald McNeal died of his wounds. . . . Indians killed and scalped Garrett Pendergrest killed or took prisoner Peter Flin. . . . Indians killed and scalped Danl Goodman wounded Capt Boone Capt Todd, Hite & Stoner . . . Barney Stagner killed & beheaded ½ mile from the Fort."

People lived every minute in fear, not knowing which would be their last. No man could milk his cow, no woman go to the well, no child play in the yard without constantly stopping to listen and peer into the gloomy forest. When Indians attacked, many had to make life-and-death choices in the blink of an eye. A man, fleeing with his old mother and baby son, saw that he couldn't carry both and dropped his boy. A young mother hiding in bushes with her children strangled her newborn to stifle its cries. When Indians surprised one settlement, those inside the stockade closed the gate while eight children were being tomahawked outside. Having to make such decisions changed the survivors for the rest of their lives.

Hard choices made for hard people. For many there were no "good" or "bad," "innocent" or "guilty" Indians. There were just Indians, and all were wild beasts to be destroyed.

This attitude dulled whites' feelings toward fellow human beings, allowing them to do terrible things. A frontiersman justified killing Indian women and children by saying "Nits make lice"; that is, the young will grow up to be heathens like their parents. Frontiersmen scalped their victims and used the hair as fringes on hunting shirts. At Harrodsburg, Indian bodies were fed to the dogs, because that was supposed to make them fierce.

WHILE SETTLERS huddled behind stockades at Boonesborough and its sister settlements, a young Virginian visited his home state, which claimed Kentucky as its backcountry. Born in 1752, George Rogers Clark was a handsome sixfooter with red hair and black eyes. Clark, like George Washington, began his career as a land surveyor. During his wilderness journeys, he came to love Kentucky and its people. He admired everything about them, their generosity, their independence, even their rough ways.

Clark had come to suggest a plan to Thomas Jefferson and other Virginia leaders. His idea was to save Kentucky by conquering the entire Northwest Territory. He'd already sent spies into the area, and they reported it undefended except for some French militia and a handful of Redcoats at Fort Detroit. Clark wanted to lead a small force undetected into the area to take the French settlements. With these secured, and backed by reinforcements from Virginia, he'd attack Fort Detroit. The Virginia legislature secretly approved his plan, giving him money for supplies and authority to recruit volunteers.

Clark started down the Ohio River with a handful of Virginia riflemen in flatboats. This was an adventure in itself, complete with rollercoaster rapids that shot them forward at dizzying speeds. As they moved downstream, they were joined by Pennsylvanians and Kentuckians, until Clark had 178 men under his command. He called them his "force of invasion," a grand name for little more than a militia company.

Clark made camp a hundred miles east of where the Ohio joins the Mississippi. There they met a party of American buffalo hunters who'd left Kaskakia eight days earlier. The French had no idea that invaders were anywhere within a thousand miles, they said. But it was best to go the remaining 125 miles overland rather than risk being seen on the Mississippi.

They reached Kaskakia toward evening on Saturday, July 4, 1778. All was well. There were no guards; indeed,

*George Rogers Clark tried to defend Kentucky by capturing British outposts further to the west.*

the townspeople were having a dance in the fort. Cautiously, Clark's men stole into town. Clark himself crawled into the fort through an open window. Following the sound of music to a large room lit with torches, he stood in the doorway, arms folded, watching the dancers. Suddenly an Indian, who'd been sitting on the floor with his back to the wall, noticed the stranger and gave a war whoop. The dancing stopped. Women screamed. Men ran toward the door. Clark just stood there. When at last he spoke, he said they could fight—if they wanted a massacre. His men were everywhere and meant to have Kaskakia, over their dead bodies if necessary. The dance broke up and everyone went home to spend a restless night.

Next morning, Clark gathered the people to announce that he served the United States. Americans would be glad to welcome them as fellow countrymen. But if they couldn't break their oath to King George, they were welcome to leave. Oh, yes, there was one more thing. Clark announced that the United States and France had signed a Treaty of Alliance. That's all the Kaskakians had to hear. They swore allegiance to the new nation, ran to the church to give thanks, and danced in the streets for joy. It wasn't long before the people of Cahokia and Vincennes did the same.

Clark's next task was to neutralize the Indians, who'd surely attack if he moved against Fort Detroit. Since his men wouldn't have a chance against thousands of well-armed braves, he decided to use his skill as an actor.

Clark called the Indians to a council at Cahokia. Braves flocked into town, curious to see Long Knife (this, because of his sword), who'd conquered the French without a shot and who seemed to fear nothing. What they didn't know was that his confidence was part of the act; for although Clark stayed alone in a house and even gave a dance, riflemen were always hidden nearby.

As the chiefs sat cross-legged around a log fire, Clark stepped into the council circle. Shadows played across his face, and for minutes that felt like hours he "spoke" only with his eyes. He stared at the chiefs, seeming to look into their very brains. When finally he spoke, it was to tell them that he came not as a talker, but as a fighter. Though his force was small, he had only to call and the warriors of the Thirteen Council Fires (the thirteen United States) would swarm across the land like locusts. He advised them, he later wrote, "to lay down their Tomahawk, and if they did not choose [to do] it to behave like Men and fight for the English as they had done; but they would see their great father [Hairbuyer Hamilton] given to the dogs to eat." They chose to make peace with Long Knife, who then settled down to await reinforcements from Virginia.

In the meantime, Hairbuyer Hamilton invited Indian chiefs to Fort Detroit to try to win back their loyalty. He fired cannon salutes, held feasts, and sang war songs with them around the council fire. Several chiefs went back on their pledges to Long Knife and smoked the war pipe with the Englishman.

Hamilton set out for Vincennes with 177 whites and 60 Indians and was joined by hundreds of braves along the way. After a six-week journey by canoe and overland, the expedition reached Vincennes on December 17, 1778, capturing the one American Clark had left there as his representative. Satisfied with his easy victory, Hamilton decided to spend the winter there. There was need to hurry now, he felt. He wanted to let news of his success spread among the tribes, who'd flock to him in the spring. By then, too, reinforcements would have arrived from Canada with artillery.

Clark was in a tight spot. With winter closing in and no reinforcements, it was clear that Hamilton would crush his force in the spring. Not only would he recapture the French towns, he'd destroy Kentucky, for wooden stockades couldn't stand up to cannon. He might even push up the Ohio River into western Pennsylvania, linking up with Joseph Brant and the Tory rangers.

Clark was an optimist by nature. He really believed that every cloud has a silver lining and that things get worse before they get better. The odds might be against him, but they might at the same time offer opportunities for the bold. Since Hamilton seemed to have everything in his favor, there was only one thing for Clark to do: attack. This was not as foolish as it sounds. He knew that Hamilton felt secure in

Vincennes, which meant he wouldn't expect an attack by a smaller force in midwinter. There was an excellent chance of catching him by surprise.

Clark left Kaskakia on one of the epic marches of American history with 180 men, half of them French volunteers, February 7, 1779. Despite snow, the going was easy during the first few days. They passed through herds of buffalo, a ready supply of fresh meat. They had no tents, but there was plenty of wood and they gathered at night around bonfires to cook their meals and sleep. To keep up their spirits, Clark gave double rations of whiskey and led them in Indian war dances.

But as they advanced, the weather became mild, turning snow to slush and melting the ice of the three rivers in their path. The Little Wabash, Embarrass, and Wabash rivers overflowed their banks, flooding hundreds of square miles of countryside. The plain became a vast lake broken by occasional hillocks that rose as tiny islands above the flood. With the grass under water, the game disappeared and Clark's men soon felt hunger gnawing at their bellies.

An ordeal began such as few soldiers have experienced. By day they slogged across the "drowned lands," as Clark called the plain. The depth of the water varied from ankle-deep to waist-deep to chin-deep. The men walked mile after mile, often falling when they stepped into submerged holes. A few rafts had been built for the heavy equipment, but each man carried his own gear. A man might walk for hours with his rifle, powder horn, and pack held over his head. His muscles ached, but he didn't dare wet the powder or the flints that set it off. At night he slept on a hillock huddled near a fire made with wet wood, wheezing and coughing from the smoke. If the hillock wasn't dry—and it usually wasn't—he slept in mud in wet clothes covered by wet blankets. The marvel of it all was that everyone remained in good health.

Clark knew that good spirits made for good health. He had a natural gift for inspiring men, and they took their

lead from him in all things. They did as he did, but they also felt as he felt. He'd march ahead, smiling, singing, joking about "land in sight!" They laughed, forgot the hardships, and sang along.

Clark once returned from scouting and, forgetting himself, looked worried. Soon everyone had a long face and began to complain. Clark realized the cause and whispered to the officers to imitate him. He gathered some water in the hollow of his palm and mixed it with gunpowder until it became black mush. He then smeared it on his face, gave a war whoop, and marched into the water without saying a word. Silently the weary men followed him. He began to sing and before long the plain echoed to their voices.

The worst part of the journey came as they neared Vincennes. Just ahead lay Horse Shoe Plain, now a lake four miles across. On the other side was a woods and beyond it the town. Before setting out on this last stage of the trip, Clark formed a rear guard with orders to shoot anyone who tried to turn back. Turn back! Not with Hairbuyer Hamilton practically in their hands! They cheered and staggered across the flooded plain. After an all-day march, they dragged themselves into the woods and saw Vincennes through the trees, February 23, 1779. Luckily, they captured some squaws paddling a canoe filled with buffalo meat. A good meal gave them energy for the task ahead.

The problem wasn't capturing Vincennes, which they did without firing a shot. The problem was the fort, whose defenders had heavy cannon mounted on the walls. The Hairbuyer thought the call to surrender a big joke. To show that he was in control, he fired a couple of cannonballs into the town, hitting the church but hurting no one.

*"Follow Me!" In February 1779, George Rogers Clark led his raiders across hundreds of square miles of flooded lands to capture British Colonel Henry Hamilton at Vincennes on the Wabash River.*

Clark's men sprang into action. Sharpshooters took cover, zeroing in on every loophole and gun port with their rifles. These openings were small, but backwoodsmen prided themselves on being able to shoot off a squirrel's head at a hundred yards. No sooner did someone prepare to fire when a rifle bullet found him. The Hairbuyer's men were in big trouble.

Suddenly a war cry burst from the nearby forest. An Indian raiding party, not knowing that Clark had taken Vincennes, was returning with American scalps dangling from sticks. They were happy as they came on, whooping, pounding their chests, and waving their trophies.

Clark and his men savored the moment; it was a rare delight for frontiersmen to catch Indians returning with scalps and they wanted to make the most of it. Clark sent out a "welcoming committee" of his own. Both groups ran toward each other, whooping and cheering, until the Indians came in range. Rifle shots brought down five, who were promptly scalped; five others were captured.

Clark had something special in store for his prisoners. They'd murdered settlers and were doomed. But his way of killing them was meant to impress the Hairbuyer and his men. The braves were seated in a circle in full view of the fort. A sergeant then stepped behind each man in turn and buried his tomahawk in his skull. One brave didn't die immediately; he took the tomahawk out of his head and handed it to the executioner for another try.

The killings done, Clark asked the Hairbuyer to meet him to discuss the situation. Hamilton was shaken by what he'd seen and horrified at the American commander's appearance; Clark had stood so close to the Indians that his face, hands, and clothes were spattered with blood. They met near a beached canoe filled with rainwater. Clark, smiling, washed his hands and face as he fixed the Englishman with his eyes.

*British Lieutenant Colonel Henry Hamilton, known as "Hairbuyer Hamilton," surrenders his sword to George Rogers Clark at Vincennes.*

He warned Hamilton that he must surrender at once or be treated as a murderer when his men stormed the fort. The Hairbuyer surrendered later that day.

Hamilton was sent to Virginia under armed guard. Virginia Governor Thomas Jefferson, normally a kindly man, made an exception in his case. He had the Hairbuyer loaded with chains and kept on short rations in a dark, damp, filthy dungeon until the end of the war. Hamilton's health was ruined, but no more than that of his victims.

Clark was eager to follow up his victory by capturing Fort Detroit. He appealed to Virginia for reinforcements, but only 150 men arrived. "At this moment," he wrote, "I would have bound myself a slave to have had five hundred men." The only thing to do was to go on the defensive and try to hold on until the end of the war.

Fort Detroit, like Fort Niagara after Sullivan's campaign, remained an enemy base of operations for three more years. During that time a number of war parties slipped past Clark's defenses, to attack the Kentucky settlements.

In August 1782, the Tory Simon Girty led three hundred braves to Brant's Station, a settlement built by relatives of Daniel Boone's wife, Rachel. Girty surrounded it at night, hoping to ambush the men when they came out to work in the morning. With the men dead, the women and children would be at the mercy of his Indians.

Somehow it was learned that raiders were hiding in the cornfields and messengers were sent to bring help from other settlements. Brant's Station was defended by sixty men, each having three rifles and a woman or boy to keep them loaded. The worst problem was lack of water. There was no well inside the stockade and the day's supply had to be brought in buckets from a nearby spring. There was no chance of beating off an attack without water.

There was only one thing to do. The defenders realized that Girty wanted to get rid of the men before attacking the fort. They also knew that he didn't know that he'd been discovered. They decided to send the women out for water as usual at sunup. There would be no exceptions: Everyone must go.

As the sun rose in the east, thirty-five wives and daughters knelt in prayer. After making their peace with God, they took their buckets and, chatting and laughing as on any normal day, walked through the gate. It was a good act, for Indians were all around the spring. Under a bush a woman saw a hand grasping a tomahawk; beyond, a teenager noticed the tips of a pair of moccasins. Calmly they went about their task and, when finished, started back along the path. Finally they were inside and the gate shut behind them. That's when the tension snapped. Women fell into the arms of their menfolk and couples burst into tears.

When no one else appeared after several hours, Girty knew he'd been tricked. He stood up and shouted his ultimatum: surrender now or die when his cannon arrived.

A youth named Aaron Reynolds returned the challenge. "I have a good-for-nothing dog named Simon Girty because he looks like you," he shouted. "Bring on your artillery if you've got any, and be damned to you! We, too, are expecting reinforcements; the whole country is marching to us, and if you and your gang of murderers stay here another day we will have your scalps drying in the sun." From behind the stockade came the sound of laughter.

Girty's men opened fire, but were no match for concealed sharpshooters. Fire arrows, one of which landed next to a baby in its cradle, were doused by alert youngsters. Next morning, all was quiet. The raiders were gone. That afternoon Daniel Boone and other commanders arrived with 180 mounted riflemen.

The Kentuckians set out after Girty, following a buffalo trace that led to the Blue Licks. Along the way they discovered plenty of footprints, campfire remains, and even blazes carved into treetrunks. Instead of scattering after the raid, the Indians had left a trail a child could follow. Why? Daniel Boone understood: They were being led into a trap.

They arrived at the Blue Licks next day, August 19, 1782.

Across the river, they saw a few dozen Indians moving about on an open ridge. Boone knew this country like the back of his hand. He warned that the area was honeycombed with ravines hidden by clumps of grass. Ambush country. Those ravines were full of Indians. He'd bet his life on it. Unfortunately, hotheads impatient for revenge ignored his pleas for caution. "Delay is cowardly!" said one commander. "Let all those who are not cowards follow me, and I will show them the Indians!" And that's exactly what he did.

The Kentuckians splashed across the shallow stream, dismounted, and advanced on foot; Boone followed, unwilling to leave even fools to their fate. Suddenly a war whoop split the air as hundreds of braves opened fire from the ravines. Caught in a cross fire, the Kentuckians fell where they stood. Their front collapsed. Panic spread as men ran for their horses, only to be overtaken by braves with tomahawks. Only Daniel Boone was able to organize a fighting retreat on the left flank. As he fell back, he heard the thud of a bullet behind him. Turning, he saw his son Israel, twenty-three, fall with blood gushing from his mouth. The Battle of the Blue Licks was over within five minutes. In this, the last action of the American Revolution, the Kentuckians had seventy-seven killed, one-third of their force, and more men than they'd lost in any other battle. But they had held the west for their country.

Britain gave up the Northwest Territory at the peace conference, extending the borders of the United States to the Great Lakes and the Mississippi. But there was never real peace west of the Alleghenies. The killings and burnings and scalpings continued year after year. Finally, during his second term as president, George Washington sent an army under General "Mad" Anthony Wayne to break the frontier tribes. He did so in August 1794. At Fallen Timbers near the present city of Toledo, Ohio, Wayne handed the tribes the worst defeat they'd ever suffered. After Fallen Timbers, the Northwest Territory lay open to white settlement and the frontier moved farther west.

## · *SEVEN* ·

---

# The Secret War

*E*VERY war is actually two wars. There is, first, the clash of armies in battle. Yet for every army in the field, there is another, secret, army behind the scenes. This army is not made up of masses of armed men, but of individuals and small groups who seldom see combat. These are the quiet warriors, the men and women who collect information about the enemy. The old saying that knowledge is power is especially true in war. Battles are decided by facts as well as force. The best generals are just gamblers, their troops blundering mobs, without information to guide planning and action.

Spying is as old as war itself. In war, as in peace, nations have secrets that must be kept. Learning these secrets is the job of the spy, or espionage agent. Spying is dangerous work and attracts people for various reasons. Greed is a powerful motive; spying for some is a cure for financial problems or a way to get rich quick. For others it is an adventure in which their skill and courage are constantly being tested.

Finally, there are the idealists. These are often the most valuable agents, because they believe in a cause and are willing to risk everything for it.

Spies are interested in anything about an enemy's abilities and intentions. Battle plans are most valuable, but also hardest to get. Almost as important is information on troop strength, battle losses, weapons, supplies, and the enemy's own agents. Army commanders must be up to date on the enemy order of battle, that is, locating each unit and learning its strength and mission. Knowing the whereabouts of enemy senior officers may help predict future actions. Naval commanders need to know about enemy ship sailings, cargoes, and destinations.

Since such information is closely guarded, spies must get into enemy territory to gather it and then bring it out. Nowadays most nations have schools to teach spying, communications, codes, use of explosives, and self-defense. Nothing like these existed in the 1700s. Spies followed certain time-tested rules, but were otherwise left to their own ingenuity and luck. The penalty for failure was severe. Today, captured spies are often exchanged. In the old days they were hung.

During the American Revolution, spies from both sides entered enemy territory in disguise. Since patrols were watchful, strangers had to have a good *cover story*, or reason for moving about in an area. A spy might be a herdsman, merchant, blacksmith, dentist—anyone who traveled for a living. The spy would then observe enemy movements, befriend soldiers, and even offer to pay them for information. British agent Ann Bates spent a whole day at Washington's White Plains headquarters disguised as a peddler, eavesdropping on officers' conversations.

There were several ways of smuggling information across enemy lines. A favorite method was the *book code*. A spy and his contact each had a copy of the same book or dictionary. The message was then written as a series of numbers: thus, 102.10.12 meant page 102, line ten, twelfth word. In *substitution ciphers*, the position of letters in the alphabet were changed. In our example the letters are reversed:

abcdefghijklmnopqrstuvwxyz
may become
zyxwvutsrqponmlkjihgfedcba

The message might then be written as a single word to confuse code-breakers. Can you read the following?

gsvvmvnbhgirpvhzgwzdm
[The enemy strikes at dawn.]

The problem with such messages is that they may be read with the help of a frequency table. In every language certain letters and letter combinations are used most frequently. In English these are e, t, a, o, n, i, r, ee, ng, th, and so on. By counting the number of times each coded letter appeared and then arranging the letters in order of frequency, one could break the code.

To confuse code-breakers further, messages were written in *stain*, invisible ink. Then, as now, messages written in certain chemicals were invisible until painted with other chemicals. If stains weren't available, an agent could always use lime juice or milk, which are developed by holding the paper over a candle flame.

Messages were passed along in several ways. A letter drop or post office might be a hollow log, an empty bottle, an old beehive—any place an agent could leave a paper for another agent, or agent's messenger, to find. An agent might also hide a message on his person, usually sewn into clothes or placed in the hollow heel of a boot. Spies still use these tried and true methods.

British agents sometimes carried messages in hollow silver bullets, which could easily be swallowed and remain inside the body without corroding. One man, when stopped by a patrol, was seen to swallow a silver bullet. The Americans forced him to vomit it up, but he grabbed the bullet and swallowed it again. An officer sternly warned that he'd be hung and the bullet cut out of his belly if he didn't vomit it up again. He did and was hung anyhow. The Americans made a sick joke about him being condemned "out of his own mouth."

BOTH SIDES during the Revolution had effective spy services. The French service was large and experienced. For nearly a century, the kings of France had filled their country with spies to keep tabs on the people. The lessons they learned were also useful in foreign espionage. After the French and Indian War, the British ambassador in Paris was kept under constant observation. Agents followed his every movement. His servants were bribed to reveal the smallest details of his life, even down to his daily breakfast menu.

French agents were active in England itself. They had plenty of money and used it freely to bribe anyone who might be helpful. There were spies listening to the gossip at the royal court. An Englishman working for France got elected to Parliament and reported on its secret debates. Other spies served in the War Office and Admiralty, which planned military and naval operations. None of these agents were caught, and we know about them only because historians have studied secret French records.

The father of American espionage was George Washington, who believed that spying was absolutely necessary to win the Revolution. "Where-ever [the enemy] Army lies," he said, "it will be of the greatest advantage to us to have spies among them." On the day after his appointment as commander in chief, June 16, 1775, he was visited by mysterious men. These men, whose names have never been revealed, became the first members of his spy service. He was well suited to be a spymaster. A tight-lipped person by nature, he knew how to keep secrets. Even his closest aides, men he trusted with his life, never learned of his deepest plans and plots.

Washington took good care of his agents. His troops might be paid in near-worthless paper money, but his agents were paid out of a small chest no one but himself could go near. The chest contained gold and silver coins. He spent $55,000 during the Revolution, a very large sum, for "secret intelligence."

The general protected the identity of his agents, always meeting them at night in his tent surrounded by his trusted Life Guards. Spies expected not only to be paid for their work, but to receive a special document after the war. That document was a kind of life insurance policy. Addressed to their neighbors, it explained that they weren't Tories, but had pretended to be to gain Tory confidence and information. Many a man was kept from a suit of tar and feathers by Washington's signature on a piece of paper.

It has been said that the Father of our Country never told a lie. True, in his private and business life he was as honest as the day is long. But where the good of his country was concerned, he showed a talent for lying and trickery. Even the best of men can't run a spy network and be truthful in all things.

Some of Washington's tricks would be envied by the head of any twentieth-century spy service. Washington understood that information could flow two ways. If agents could get good information from the British, they could also feed them bad information so they'd make mistakes.

After the Battle of Germantown, for example, Washington wanted to conceal his army's weakness from Sir William Howe. One day a merchant appeared at headquarters with a tale of how the Redcoats had mistreated him. The general had expected Howe to send a spy to learn his strength. Very well, he'd let him do just that. Instead of arresting the "merchant," he had him wait in an office with reports open on a desk. Of course the "merchant" read the reports and was gone next morning with news that the Americans were stronger than expected. But what neither he nor his master knew was that the reports were fakes prepared especially for British eyes.

Washington also planted false papers on the enemy. After the Battle of Monmouth, he decided to trick Sir Henry

Clinton into believing that he would attack New York City in order to make him cancel plans for attacks elsewhere. Washington prepared several letters to American commanders hinting at an assault on New York. He prepared them carefully, lovingly, relishing the idea of fooling the Englishman. But how to get these letters into Clinton's hands? He couldn't just mail them to "Sir Henry Clinton, Army Headquarters, New York City."

Washington had a messenger brought to his tent. When he gave the man the letters and told him the route he must follow, he turned pale. "Why, General, I shall be taken, if I go through the Clove!" said he. Washington looked him in the eye and, stamping his foot, growled: "Your duty, sir, is not to talk, but to obey!" He'd deliberately sent the messenger out to be captured, knowing he wouldn't be treated as a spy so long as he was in uniform. The trick worked and Clinton prepared for an attack that never came.

Yet not all of Washington's plans succeeded. In September 1776, after the Battle of Long Island and before the loss of New York City, he wanted information about enemy positions on Long Island. Captain Nathan Hale, a twenty-four-year-old Connecticut schoolmaster, volunteered for the mission. It was his first espionage assignment and, as things turned out, also his last.

Hale landed by boat on Long Island's North Shore with his Yale diploma in his pocket. The diploma was essential to his cover, for he pretended to be a teacher wandering the countryside in search of a job for the fall. But except for his cover story, his mission was an example of how not to do undercover work. He had facial scars that had been caused by exploding gunpowder, which guaranteed that once seen he'd never be forgotten. He had no contacts among patriots in British territory. Nor did he have stains, forcing him to keep written notes, a sure giveaway if captured.

After landing on September 12, Hale set out to observe British positions. Three days later, however, his information became useless after Lord Howe captured New York. His mission was over and no one would have said a word against him had he rejoined his unit. Instead, he gave himself a new mission. Somehow he got across the East River and began spying on the British army in New York. During the next week he passed through the enemy lines, making notes and drawings of their positions.

No one today knows how Hale was discovered. All we can say is that the British arrested him, and, when they found his notes, he confessed to being a spy. Ordinarily, even confessed spies were given a trial before being condemned. But Lord Howe was too busy for such formalities and ordered Hale executed the next morning, September 22, 1776.

Before sunrise, with death near, he asked to speak to a clergyman and to have a Bible during his final minutes on earth. His requests were brushed aside. He was taken to the place of execution, now the corner of First Avenue and Fifty-first Street. There he found a ladder standing against a tree; a noose hung from one of the branches. His hands were tied, the noose tightened around his neck, and he was made to climb the ladder. He told the few Redcoats who'd come to see his end that life is short and they must be ready to meet death at any moment. His last words were: "I only regret that I have but one life to lose for my country." Then the executioner pulled away the ladder. When his body had hung there for several hours, British troops placed a sign on the tree: GEORGE WASHINGTON.

One of Washington's best agents was Lydia Darragh of Philadelphia. This quiet, fifty-two-year-old mother of nine was a staunch patriot. When the British occupied her city in 1777, she found herself living across the street from Sir William Howe's headquarters. She looked sharply and listened carefully. Whenever she learned anything interesting, she sent it to Washington, whose army was camped at nearby Whitemarsh.

Lydia's spying was a family affair, so few outside it knew of her work. Mother collected the information. Father, a teacher, wrote it in shorthand on the thinnest paper. Young

*"I only regret that I have but one life to lose for my country." Taken as a spy in New York City, Connecticut schoolmaster Nathan Hale, 21, was hung by the British on Sunday, September 22, 1776. Lord Howe ordered the execution without the formality of a trial.*

John, fourteen, smuggled the paper out of town in a hollow coat button. He delivered the button to brother Charles, an army lieutenant, who translated the shorthand and sent the information to the general.

On December 2, a British staff officer glittering in scarlet and gold came to the Darraghs' front door. Asking for the lady of the house, he explained that headquarters was crowded and he needed her back room for an officers' meeting that night. She was to set a cozy fire in the fireplace and send the family to bed before his guests arrived at seven o'clock. That was a strange request, she thought. Clearly, the officers wanted to discuss something important.

That night she lay in bed without sleeping. All was quiet except for the murmur of voices from the back of the house. At last curiosity got the better of fear. Slipping out of bed, she walked barefoot to a closet next to the meeting room. Only a thin board covered with wallpaper stood between her and the officers.

What she heard set her mind reeling. Lord Howe was planning a surprise attack on Whitemarsh. She took that very personally, for not only was her son there, but dozens of other young men she knew. She had to warn Washington.

With that thought in mind, she returned to bed. Moments later a door slammed and she heard the tread of boots coming down the hall. They stopped outside her door and someone knocked. It was the staff officer come to tell her to lock the front door and put out the fire. But instead of answering immediately, she let him knock several times to give the impression that he'd wakened her from a deep sleep. Those extra knocks were to save her life.

Next morning, Lydia set out to buy flour at a mill outside town. She told no one of her true mission, not even her husband, for she wanted him to be able to tell the "truth" if questioned by the British. Arriving at the mill, she left her sack to be filled and continued down the road toward the American lines. Sure enough, she met a patrol led by a colonel she knew. Washington had Howe's plans within the hour and was waiting for him when he marched out of Philadelphia soon afterward. Having lost the element of surprise, Howe retreated in humiliation. And anger. Any fool could see that his plans had leaked.

A few days later, the staff officer visited Lydia a second time. He questioned her closely, asking if any of her family had left their beds during the meeting. Calmly, truthfully, she said her family had slept till morning. As for Lydia herself, the officer recalled that he had to knock several times to waken her, so she couldn't have eavesdropped. Lydia, who hated lying, saw no need to give him more information than he'd requested.

THE BRITISH SECRET SERVICE, created in the 1500s during the reign of Queen Elizabeth I, is Europe's oldest. During the American Revolution, George III ran it personally. His Majesty spent hours each day reading reports of agents in the field and planning future missions. France swarmed with his agents, who were in turn pursued by French agents. Spies were so busy, people said, that you couldn't talk to a friend in a café without someone trying to listen.

The British were particularly interested in the three American representatives, or commissioners, in France: Benjamin Franklin, Silas Deane, and Arthur Lee. They surrounded them with a net of secret agents. Butlers, maids, cooks, coachmen, gardeners, tradesmen—all worked for the Secret Service, although none knew the others' identity. The Secret Service also employed double agents, people who pretend to spy for one side but who really work for the enemy.

Britain's most valuable spy was Edward Bancroft, an American scientist and writer in Paris who always seemed to need money. The Secret Service began paying him as a *sleeper* in 1773; that is, one who lived normally among the enemy, building up trust and waiting for the right moment to act. The Secret Service knew that Bancroft would have an important post if war broke out with the colonies. It ordered him to join the patriots, gain their confidence, and await further orders.

That was a wise decision, for when the Revolution began, Bancroft became secretary to the American commissioners. They liked him, trusted him, and let him copy their most secret letters in his neat handwriting. But what they didn't know was that he always made an extra copy, which he left in an empty bottle hidden in a hollow tree in a Paris garden. A messenger took the papers, replacing them with money and instructions for the spy. Because of him, British frigates captured scores of ships bound for the United States with war materials. Bancroft's treason remained undiscovered for sixty years. Benjamin Franklin thought him a good friend until the day he died.

Franklin himself was a spy's delight. He hadn't the slightest notion of security. Important papers lay strewn on his desk, open for anyone to read. When a friend begged him to be more careful, he replied that he was an honest man who had nothing to be ashamed of, and therefore had nothing to hide. Codes confused him; he couldn't remember which code went with which message, nor did he have the patience to decode long messages. As a result, the British stole secrets from under his very nose.

Although Franklin trusted Bancroft, he knew the British were spying on him and used that knowledge against them. Franklin, world famous as an inventor and scientist (he'd proven that lightning was electricity), left clues that he was turning his genius to making war machines. Soon, London learned that he had set up giant mirrors on the French coast to reflect the sun's rays across the English Channel to burn the British fleet in its harbors. Other spies reported that he'd invented a huge chain connected to an electrical machine to be stretched from France to England: When the machine was turned on, the chain would electrocute the whole island. We know these ideas were nonsense, but they made the British waste time and money trying to find out more about nothing.

Franklin was also a master at issuing fake news stories that couldn't be traced to him. A letter he wrote using the name of a New England militia captain described the capture of a shipment of scalps sent to the British in Canada by the Seneca Indians. "The packages contained 954 salted scalps of [American] men, women, and children. Each scalp was elaborately marked with symbols indicating the age and sex of the person, where they were killed, and how." The letter appeared in newspapers throughout Europe, shocking people at the cruelty of Britain's "savage" allies. During the next two centuries, this story found its way into American schoolbooks, keeping alive the hatreds of that terrible time.

British commanders in America knew the importance of having good spies and plenty of them. At the same time Edward Bancroft became a sleeper, General Gage was building a spy network in Massachusetts. No one today knows these spies' identities, for code letters instead of names were used even in his secret papers. But they certainly did important work. It is no accident that he knew weapons were being stored at Concord; indeed, when the Redcoats went to seize them, they knew in which houses they were hidden. Gage failed, not because the Minutemen fought back, but because patriot spies learned of the raid in time to have the weapons moved to safety.

The discovery of Gage's best agent shocked patriots everywhere. One day in September 1775, a young woman visited Godfrey Wenwood at his bakery in Newport, Rhode Island. They had once been sweethearts but hadn't seen each other for some time. Now she had a special favor to ask. People were used to seeing him peddling his goods and buying flour in Newport and the neighboring towns. Could he deliver a letter to a certain Tory? Wenwood hesitated, but gave in after a little coaxing.

Wenwood was no Tory and certainly no traitor. The fact that the woman had a letter for a Tory and wouldn't discuss its contents made him suspicious. His curiosity aroused, he opened the letter after she returned to her home near Boston. He found three pages covered, not with words, but groupings of letters that made no sense at all. Even a humble baker knew a code when he saw one. Immediately he set out for the American camp outside Boston, where he asked to see George Washington in person.

Washington wasted no time in getting to the bottom of the mystery. He asked Wenwood for the woman's address and sent a squad of cavalry to bring her to headquarters. Washington and several officers questioned her until she admitted that the Tory was supposed to pass on the letter to the captain of a British warship. It had been given to her by the man she loved: Dr. Benjamin Church.

The questioners could hardly believe their ears. At forty-one, Dr. Church was not only a respected surgeon, but a writer, poet, and speaker; he'd delivered the memorial oration on the third anniversary of the Boston Massacre. Sam and John Adams had known him for years. And now he was Director General of Hospitals, the Continental Army's chief medical officer. In that post he could visit any unit at any time; he was always informed about upcoming operations in order to prepare for the wounded. He was the last person you'd suspect of being a traitor.

The general had the doctor brought to headquarters for questioning. He was all smiles, with an answer for every question. The coded letter? Oh, yes, it was his. It was to his brother in occupied Boston. A man can write to his brother, can't he? Unfortunately, the letter was about family business and he had no intention of handing over the key to the code.

Washington turned the letter over to three soldiers skilled at code-breaking. It was in a simple code, which they easily broke. The letter said nothing about Church family affairs. It did, however, give details about the strength, supplies, and positions of the army besieging Boston.

News of Dr. Church's treason spread like wildfire. "I stand astonished," said John Adams. "A man of genius, of learning, of family, of character, a writer of liberty songs, and good ones, too. . . . Good God! What shall we say of human nature! What shall we say of American patriots!" Men who'd been friends of Dr. Church for years felt hurt and betrayed. If patriots couldn't trust one of their own, they wondered who they could trust.

Washington wanted to hang the doctor as a warning to others. Luckily for Dr. Church, Congress had never imagined that anyone connected with the army could commit treason. According to army regulations, the most serious punishment a court-martial could order was loss of pay for two months and thirty-nine lashes. The death penalty was quickly approved for traitors, but too late to hang this traitor. He was locked in a dungeon and forbidden to write or speak to anyone except his jailers. After two years, his health broke and Congress decided to show mercy. Dr. Church was put on a ship bound for the West Indies and warned never to return. There must have been a storm at sea, for neither he nor the ship were ever seen again.

Meantime, other agents were plotting against George Washington himself. The British Secret Service realized that the outcome of the Revolution depended on him more than any other person. If he could be "removed," the Revolution would collapse like a house of cards. Thus, he was not only spied upon, but became the target of other types of secret operations.

British agents began a campaign of character assassination against the commander in chief; that is, they tried to destroy people's confidence in him. They spread rumors that he might betray the Revolution in return for money and a duke's title. The Secret Service also forged a set of letters printed under the title *Letters of George Washington and his Friends in 1776*. In these letters "Washington" spoke highly of George III, "my King," and referred to Congress as a pack of fools and "puppets." Some people were fooled by this hoax, but most simply chuckled.

There was nothing funny about the next scheme. In June of 1776, British agents organized about twenty Tories into a special strike force. With the aid of several members of Washington's Life Guard, who'd been bribed, they planned to break into his New York headquarters. They'd kidnap the general and hustle him aboard one of Black Dick Howe's warships, which would take him to England to stand trial for high treason. If for any reason he couldn't be taken away, he was to be killed on the spot.

America owes a lot to Isaac Ketchum, a thief who happened to be in the New York City jail at this time. One day Ketchum overheard gossip about a plot against the general. Now, Ketchum was no patriot, but he knew a good thing when he saw it. He went to the authorities and asked for a deal: his freedom in return for spying on his fellow prisoners. Ketchum was doing just that when a new man was brought in a few days later. He was Sergeant Thomas Hickey of the

Life Guard, who'd been arrested for counterfeiting. Hickey couldn't keep his mouth shut, and before long began bragging about his Tory friends and their plans.

Little is known about what happened next. All we can say for sure is that Ketchum betrayed Hickey and that the Tories escaped before it was too late. Hickey and three other members of the Life Guard were brought to trial. The three gave evidence against the sergeant, which probably saved their lives. Washington, however, decided to make an example of Hickey. Twenty thousand people turned out to watch him swing from a gallows set up in Bowery Lane. Hickey's fate must have frightened British agents, for there were no more plots against the general's life.

SERGEANT HICKEY and his friends weren't the only American soldiers corrupted with bribes. One of the enemy's most ambitious plots was the idea of Major John Andre, Sir Henry Clinton's chief of intelligence. Andre was a remarkable person. Born in 1751, he was a gentle, lovable man who wrote poetry and enjoyed putting on plays for brother officers. Always cheerful and polite, he had a way of making others want to be his friend.

When Andre took over as intelligence chief, he began a list of American generals who might be open to bribery. None were. Andre would have liked to bribe one man in particular: Major General Benedict Arnold. But he had done so much for his country that Andre didn't include him on the list. There was no point even in thinking about bribing such a man. Little did he expect that Arnold would soon approach him with an offer of treason.

Despite his success and fame, Arnold was an unhappy man. He seems always to have been unhappy. He was haunted by the memory of his father, also named Benedict, a merchant who'd fallen on hard times. When his business failed, the old man became a drunkard. Many a time his son had to help him stagger home to the sound of neighbors' jeers and laughter. These experiences may explain the boy's, and then the man's, desire to excel in everything. Being better than others helped overcome the shame his father had brought upon the family. As a teenager, he was a daredevil who enjoyed risking his life. Once, at a flour mill, he startled friends by grabbing one of the arms of the waterwheel and letting it carry him into the air and then under the rushing stream. As an adult, he led desperate charges into enemy positions.

Arnold was recovering from his second painful leg wound when Philadelphia was recaptured. Washington, wanting to reward his courage, made him the city's military governor until he was ready for active duty. That was a decision he'd bitterly regret.

As soon as Arnold became governor, he began spending more money than he earned. He'd suffered a great deal for his country and was determined to enjoy life at its expense. He rented a big house, drove in a fancy coach, and gave banquets for Philadelphians known to have Tory friends. In order to pay for these pleasures, he used his office for shady business deals. Arnold bought goods with government money, sold them, and kept the profits. He had his goods hauled in army wagons and dealt with Tories. Officers did not approve of his life-style. "Money is this man's god," wrote Colonel John Brown, "and to get enough of it he would sacrifice his country." Criticism grew until he resigned as governor in March 1779. He was angry, vengeful, and looking for a chance to do mischief. It came quickly enough.

Meantime, Arnold, whose first wife had died leaving him with three children, began to court Margaret Shippen. Margaret, or Peggy, as friends called her, came from a wealthy Philadelphia family. A lively, pretty girl, she'd been popular with young British officers during the occupation. Although Arnold was twice her age—he thirty-seven, she eighteen— she fell in love with the famous general and married him in April 1779. A few weeks later, he sent a secret letter to British headquarters in New York. It was addressed to his bride's dear friend: Major John Andre.

That letter was a bombshell. In it, America's greatest

*Before he became a traitor, Major General Benedict Arnold was one of the Continental Army's finest fighting officers.*

hero next to Washington himself offered to betray his country. In return for treason, Arnold wanted a promise of British protection for himself and his family. He expected, in addition, to be made a general in the British army and sent to fight the rebels. But most of all, he demanded money. Lots of money.

After exchanging a dozen letters written in dictionary code, it was agreed that he'd be paid according to the value of his information. The British wanted to know such things as American plans, decisions of war councils, troop movements, and the locations of ammunition dumps that might easily be raided. But they would be happiest, and pay most, if Arnold became commander of West Point and surrendered it during a "surprise" attack. West Point, now home to the United States Military Academy, was a real prize. The fortress overlooks a point where the Hudson River narrows and flows between steep hills. As long as it was in American hands, no enemy warship could pass through the channel. But if the British captured it, they could go as far as Albany, cutting

New York State in half and menacing western New England.

Although annoyed at Arnold's misconduct in Philadelphia, Washington still respected his fighting ability. When he asked for a new command, the general promised him the left wing of the Continental Army, a post of honor, in the next campaign. Arnold, who was still hobbling around, said he wasn't up to anything so strenuous. Until he recovered, he needed a quiet post, like West Point. Washington said it was a post far below his abilities, but if that's what he wanted, it was his.

Now the traitor began earning his money. Quietly, in his own soldier's way, he weakened the fortress. Needed repairs weren't made. Defenses were strengthened where they'd be unnecessary and weakened in key locations. As in Philadelphia, Arnold used the supplies for his own profit. Thousands of dollars' worth of pork, salt, and wine were sold and the money pocketed by the commander. By early September 1780, all that remained was for him to meet Andre to hand over plans of West Point and work out details of the attack. Already American spies were reporting that Clinton's troops were ready to move, although their destination was top secret.

On the night on September 20, a boat cast off from the frigate *Vulture*. Moving swiftly, its muffled oars making silvery ripples, it approached the Hudson shore near Haverstraw, thirteen miles below West Point. A man stepped ashore, shrouded in a hooded blue cloak that barely hid a scarlet uniform. Another man waited on horseback near a clump of elms. He wore a blue uniform.

Andre and Arnold sat among the elms in the moonlight, discussing their business and going over plans of West Point. They were so absorbed in their work that they lost track of time. Hours passed, and, by the time they finished, it was too late for the Englishman to return to his ship. Yet there was nothing to fear, for Arnold knew a Tory farmer nearby who'd put them up for the night.

Next morning, they decided that it was too dangerous

for Andre to try to get back aboard the *Vulture*. He would have to cross to the Hudson's east bank at King's Ferry and make his way back to the British lines by way of White Plains. But since he'd have to cross American territory, he mustn't risk capture by wearing his uniform. Andre put on civilian clothes and hid the plans in his boot, together with notes in Arnold's handwriting. That was the mistake that would cost him his life. If he'd been captured in uniform, the Americans would have had to treat him as a prisoner of war. But capture in civilian clothes with secret papers meant that he was a spy, and spying meant death.

Andre was able to take the ferry across the river and ride south on a borrowed horse. The hours must have passed slowly for him. His path was filled with danger, yet each mile brought him closer to safety. As he neared Tarrytown, only six miles from his destination, three men stepped from the woods. Although they were militiamen, their real business in the woods was robbery; this was a poor part of New York State and men got money as best they could. They ordered Andre to dismount and began going through his pockets. Had they found money, they might have let him go. But finding nothing, they looked further—in his boots. That's when they discovered the hidden papers.

The three robbers huddled together, discussing what to do next. Why should a lone traveler have such papers in his boot? Clearly, this was something they couldn't handle. They made Andre remount and took him to the American post at North Castle (now North White Plains).

Lieutenant Colonel John Jameson was the officer in charge at North Castle. Had Jameson done things his way, both the spy and the traitor might easily have escaped. After questioning Andre, he sent him to Arnold under guard, together with a letter explaining what had happened. The papers were sent to Washington, who was to inspect West Point after having breakfast at Arnold's headquarters.

Fortunately, Major Benjamin Tallmadge, Washington's chief of secret operations, came by on a scouting mission.

Tallmadge smelled a rat. Only a few people had access to plans of West Point, and the prisoner wasn't one of them. If he had them, it must be because a high-ranking officer gave them to him. And besides, what was he doing with papers in Benedict Arnold's handwriting? Could Arnold be a traitor? Tallmadge didn't know, but he intended to find out. He persuaded Jameson to have Andre brought back until the matter could be cleared up. Jameson, however, insisted that Arnold, his commanding officer, be informed of the capture.

The table was set at Arnold's headquarters across the river from West Point when a messenger brought word that Washington had been delayed and that breakfast should be served without him. Moments later, another messenger appeared with Jameson's letter. Arnold read it, ordered his barge to be made ready on the river, and had a few words with Peggy. Then, saying that he'd been called to West Point on important business, he left the house. In less than an hour, he was aboard the *Vulture* and bound for New York.

Meantime, Washington arrived, ate breakfast, and left for West Point. The place was quiet—too quiet. There were no cannon salutes to greet him, and Arnold was nowhere to be found. No one had seen him that day. Washington made his inspection and returned to Arnold's headquarters late in the afternoon, just as Jameson's second messenger rode up with the stranger's papers. He understood at once that Arnold had turned traitor. Calmly, showing not the slightest emotion, he issued orders for his arrest. At last he left the house with Lafayette. When they were alone, out of sight and hearing, he threw his arms around the Frenchman's neck and burst into tears.

Major Andre realized he was doomed during the boat ride to his trial at Tappan, New York. He asked his escort, Major Tallmadge, if he thought he'd be hung as a spy. Tallmadge thought for a moment, then told of a dear friend he'd had at Yale College named Nathan Hale. "Do you remember [him]?" Tallmadge asked.

*Major John Andre made this pen-and-ink sketch of himself while awaiting execution as a spy.*

"Yes," said Andre. "He was hanged as a spy, but you surely do not consider his case and mine alike."

"Precisely similar," the American replied, "and similar will be your fate."

Andre was found guilty of espionage by a panel of fourteen generals. In the days before his execution, he won his captors' sympathy and respect. Everyone knew that he had entered the American lines as a soldier in uniform and not as a spy. Still, the rules of war were clear and he'd die for his mistake. Yet he took the court's decision calmly, bravely, the way he believed a soldier should. Major Tallmadge came to love him as a younger brother. When he was hung on October 2, 1780, many onlookers cried. The British received the news of his death with tears and shouts of outrage. The streets of New York echoed to soldiers chanting: "Andre!

*In this parade, an effigy of a two-faced Benedict Arnold is shown in league with the devil.*

Andre! Vengeance with the bayonet upon those Sons of Rebellion!"

Arnold made more money out of the war than any American soldier. He got over six thousand pounds for attempting to betray West Point, a life pension of five hundred pounds for Peggy, and one hundred pounds for each of her five children; the three sons of his first marriage became officers in the British army, although the youngest was only nine. In addition, King George gave him 13,500 acres of land in Canada. The full value of his benefits totaled over $100,000 in today's money.

Arnold received the rewards of treason but little else. Younger British officers, who'd loved Andre, blamed their new brigadier general for his death and refused to serve under him. There is a story that, when he visited London, he was hissed in the streets. Even Englishmen not sympa-

thetic to the Revolution refused to have anything to do with a traitor.

Benedict Arnold became the most hated person in American history. He was hanged and burned in effigy in cities across the land. Parades were held in which the devil was shown whispering in his ear. Nowhere was the hatred deeper than in his home town of Norwich, Connecticut. A mob stormed the local cemetery and destroyed the gravestones of his father and a brother, who had died in infancy before the traitor's birth, simply because their first names were also Benedict.

Once his tears dried, Washington felt a hatred for Arnold such as he could never feel for any other human being. Vowing to bring the traitor to justice, he ordered Major "Light-Horse" Harry Lee, a fellow Virginian, to have him kidnapped. Lee selected Sergeant John Champe to do the job. Champe, an experienced combat veteran, was a resourceful man. He "deserted" the American army in full view of a British patrol and was brought to New York. After an interview with Sir Henry Clinton, whom he told of countless Americans who wanted to desert, he was assigned to Arnold's regiment.

Champe studied the traitor's habits carefully. He learned that Arnold always took an evening walk in the garden behind his headquarters before going to bed. The sergeant, aided by three American agents, planned to grab him, tie and gag him, and row him across the Hudson to the New Jersey shore. If Arnold struggled, he was to knock him out but not kill him even if that meant he escaped. "His public punishment," said Washington, "is the sole object in view."

Once again, however, Arnold's luck held. On the night before the kidnapping attempt, he was ordered to lead a seaborne raid into Virginia. America's greatest traitor survived the war and died in 1801, after losing most of his money in bad business deals. He is buried in a tiny cemetery in a rundown section of London.

---

# EIGHT

# The World Turned
# Upside Down

$S$IR Henry Clinton was bored
and frustrated. Ever since the Battle of Monmouth in 1778,
the war had come to a standstill in the North. His army
was bottled up in New York City, as General Gage's army
had been bottled up in Boston after Bunker Hill. The British
position was too strong to be stormed, but their force was
too weak to risk a decisive battle with George Washington's.
Thus, New York became a prison in which Clinton amused
himself by "fox hunting." A cavalryman would race through
the streets trailing a bone on a rope, followed by a yelping
dog, while the general and his staff galloped after them shouting, "Tally Ho!"

But the war couldn't be won by chasing dogs. To win,
Clinton believed that a new front had to be opened in the
South. Although large, the South was a thinly settled region.
Still, it was vital to the rebel cause. The tobacco raised there

allowed Congress to buy foreign war supplies on credit. The cities of New England and the middle states, cut off from the outside world by the British fleet, received much of their food from its farms. Losing these resources would be a crippling blow to the rebels. Besides, the South was supposed to be filled with Tories eager to join in a crusade against the rebels. A British invasion would bring the southern Tories into the fight. From then on it would be easy to seize Georgia, the Carolinas, and Virginia, attacking Washington's army through the "back door."

A start had already been made with the capture of Savannah, Georgia, in the winter of 1778. This was followed the next March by an assault on Charleston, South Carolina, the best seaport south of Philadelphia. The attack was carried out by a hundred vessels and 8,700 troops led by Clinton in person. An earlier attack in 1776 had failed, but this time the fleet forced its way past the harbor forts to bombard the city from the sea while the army cut it off by land.

General Benjamin Lincoln defended Charleston with 5,500 troops. They fought bravely and well, but against impossible odds. The British landed siege guns and began to tear the place apart. The sky was streaked with red-hot cannonballs. Bursting shells showered the earth with silvery fragments of metal. At last Lincoln surrendered after a six-week siege. Not until the fall of Bataan in the Philippines in 1942 would so many American soldiers be captured at one time.

Lord Cornwallis, who took command when Clinton returned to his New York headquarters, lost no time in following up the Charleston victory. He sent fast-moving cavalry units inland to raid plantations. In one place after another, they

*Lord Charles Cornwallis commanded British forces during the campaign in Virginia and the Carolinas. After the American Revolution, he went on to a successful career in India. From a painting by Sir W. Beechley.*

arrested those sympathetic to Congress and terrorized civilians.

Even women weren't safe. Eliza Wilkinson remembered how sweaty, rough-looking men rode up to her plantation house in a cloud of dust. "The horses of the inhuman Britons . . . seemed to tear up the earth, and the riders at the same time bellowing out the most horrid curses imaginable . . . which chilled my whole frame." They broke down the front door, shouting, "Where're these women rebels?" Eliza was robbed of everything valuable, including the dresses out of her closet and the buckles off her shoes. When she begged to be allowed to keep her wedding ring, a red-faced brute put a pistol up to her face and swore he'd pull the trigger if she didn't give it up instantly. Luckily, they didn't burn her plantation, as they did others in the neighborhood.

But not all Southerners dreaded Cornwallis's raiders. The plantation slaves welcomed them as liberators. As early as 1775, the British announced that any slave who escaped from a rebel master was automatically free. That took a lot of courage, for runaways were punished harshly. Recaptured slaves might be whipped, branded, sold to West Indian sugar plantations where most died of overwork, or hung. Yet the desire to be free was stronger than any fear, and thousands joined the British wherever they appeared, including some slaves from Mount Vernon. Unfortunately, the offer of freedom applied only to runaways. Slaves taken during raids on plantations were treated as ordinary loot and sold for their captors' profit.

Black people served the British in many ways. Black women followed the army, doing camp chores alongside Redcoats' wives. Black men enlisted in British regiments, knowing that capture meant certain death. Others served as spies and guides; at Savannah, Quamino Dolly led British troops through a swamp to the rear of the rebel positions, enabling them to capture the town easily. Most blacks, however, never saw combat but used the skills learned in slavery to help the British. Thousands worked as axmen, ditch diggers, road builders, and as skilled carpenters and blacksmiths. Although several hundred free blacks joined the Continental Army, they were never allowed to serve in the South, for fear of setting a "bad example" for the slaves.

NEW YORK, Pennsylvania, and southern Tories, organized into Tarleton's Loyal Legion, were the most feared raiders in the South. The Legion's commander and only British officer was Colonel Banastre Tarleton, twenty-six, a handsome man who liked skintight uniforms, high boots, and bearskin hats. Yet this dandy was a hell-for-leather cavalryman who was happiest in battle. Clever and cruel, Tarleton wanted to spread terror so that Americans wouldn't dare resist him.

His chance came on May 29, 1780, two weeks after the fall of Charleston. Colonel Abraham Buford was leading nearly four hundred Virginia Continentals toward the city when he learned of its capture. Buford turned back, but Tarleton's cavalrymen caught up with them in the Waxhaws wilderness near the North Carolina border.

Tarleton's Loyal Legion came on at a gallop, cheering and shouting as if nothing could stop them. The Virginians held their ground, turning away the first charge and sending Tarleton hurtling to the ground when his horse was shot from under him. The colonel was furious at losing his favorite mount, which he valued more than rebel lives; so furious, in fact, that he did nothing to prevent the tragedy that followed.

The Loyal Legion charged a second time, breaking through the rebel line. Seeing that further resistance was useless, Colonel Buford ordered his men to lay down their weapons and sent someone forward with a white surrender flag. Tarleton ignored the flag, and the man carrying it was shot in cold blood. That was the signal for his dismounted troopers to open fire and charge with bayonets while mounted men plowed into the huddled crowd with sabers. "No quarter!" they shouted. "No mercy!"

Now began a massacre of Americans by Americans. For

*Colonel Banastre Tarleton was a skilled, cruel cavalryman whom patriots called "Butcher." This is an engraving of the painting by Sir Joshua Reynolds, which was done in 1782.*

fifteen minutes, Tories stabbed and hacked at the defenseless Continentals, literally cutting them to pieces. No one was spared. Tories went over the ground, plunging bayonets into anyone who showed signs of life. Where the dead and wounded had fallen one on top of the other, Tories used bayonets as pitchforks, throwing off the topmost bodies to reach those beneath. By the time order was restored, 113 Virginians were dead and another 150 so badly wounded that they were left to die on the battlefield.

Soon Southerners were speaking of "Tarleton's quarter," war without mercy, through clenched teeth. People called him "Bloody Ban," "Butchering Ban," and "Barbarous Ban." Tarleton, however, didn't care what people called him, so long as he struck terror into their hearts. But he also inspired hatred—a fierce hatred that cried for revenge.

General Horatio Gates, the new commander in the South, tried to repeat his Saratoga victory at Camden, South Carolina, on August 16, 1780. But that was not to be, because everything went wrong from the moment he arrived. Gates's troops were walking skeletons, who'd been getting along for weeks on green corn and nearly raw meat. The night before the battle, the general issued each man a pint of watered-down molasses. That alone was enough to cause defeat. By morning, half the army had diarrhea and cramps that felt as if their guts were tied in knots. They were in no condition to meet Cornwallis's veterans.

The Battle of Camden began badly for the Americans and quickly became a disaster. Bloody Ban Tarleton's cavalry broke their line, opening the way for the Redcoats and their bayonets. The Americans might have recovered, had their general kept his head. But Gates panicked. He leaped on a fast horse and galloped away, out of the war and into disgraced retirement.

Having crushed the last American army in South Carolina, Cornwallis decided to use Camden as the jumping-off point for an invasion of North Carolina. The British advanced in three columns. Cornwallis and Tarleton led the center

*The Battle of Camden, South Carolina, August 16, 1780. When the British saw that they couldn't win the war in the North, they decided to try to break the Revolution by invading the South. Camden, like many other battles, was a British victory, although they could never deal the knockout blow.*

and southern columns, with Ferguson's Americans moving far inland on the left wing. The only Englishman in this thousand-man regiment was its commander, Major Patrick Ferguson.

We last met Major Ferguson at Brandywine, where he prevented a sniper from shooting George Washington in the back. Despite his gallantry there, Ferguson could be as ruthless as Bloody Ban himself. During his march northward, his men looted and burned patriots' houses, work that gave them much pleasure. Yet they weren't so happy after news of their actions traveled over the Blue Ridge Mountains into what is now Tennessee. Soon bands of "overmountain" men from the western settlements were giving Ferguson's patrols painful lessons in bushwhacking. Ferguson was furious and sent a warning that unless the ambushes stopped he'd cross the mountains to hang the settlers and burn their farms.

Overmountain men didn't take kindly to threats. A threat, to them, was a challenge to fight, and in a fight they always tried to land the first blow. No sooner did Ferguson's message arrive, than riders set out to rouse the settlements. Within days, over a thousand men were streaming across the Blue Ridge. They were led by experienced Indian fighters such as "Nolichucky Jack" Sevier and Colonel William Campbell, a raw-boned giant with fists big as hams. Each man was mounted and carried a long rifle. He wore boots, a fringed buckskin hunting shirt, and a coonskin cap. He carried his own rations, a bag of corn sweetened with maple syrup, and could fight for weeks on this and a canteen of water now and then.

Major Ferguson had no intention of running from these "rabble," as he called them. He took up a position at Kings Mountain on the border of the two Carolinas, a flat-topped hill rising sixty feet above the surrounding plain, its steep wooded sides strewn with boulders. Kings Mountain was a natural fortress, and Ferguson felt sure he could hold it against "God Almighty and all the rebels out of Hell." He was wrong.

The overmountain men arrived on the morning of October 7, 1780, and got down to business. Gathering in groups, they listened to pep talks by their commanders. Private James Collins, sixteen, remembered his commander telling all cowards to leave immediately, so as not to infect the others with their cowardice. Young Collins was scared, and would have liked to run away, but couldn't bear the thought of being known as a coward for the rest of his life. Swallowing hard, he made up his mind that, whatever happened, he'd act "like a man." When the speeches ended, the commanders gave the day's password: *Buford*. Collins and his comrades then put four or five bullets into their mouths, to quench thirst and make reloading easier, and started up the hillside.

Ferguson's Americans opened fire, but the overmountain men knew how to take cover. They moved like Indians, darting from rock to rock, tree to tree, stopping only to fire, reload, and fire again. As they reached the hilltop, Colonel Campbell's voice boomed over the cracking of the rifles: "Here they are, boys! Shout like hell and fight like devils!"

That's just what they did. They penned the Tories at the center of the hilltop, firing as quickly as they could. With men dropping all around, several Tories raised white surrender flags, but Major Ferguson cut them down as soon as they appeared. He fought bravely, trying to rally his men, until shot from the saddle.

Ferguson's death ended the Battle of Kings Mountain—as far as the Tories were concerned. Yet they were mistaken if they expected their surrender flags to be honored immediately. Too much blood lay between the two sides for that to happen. Now that the overmountain men had them in their power, they wanted revenge. As the Tories huddled around their surrender flags, the overmountain men's anger got out of control. Shouting *"Buford! Buford! Tarleton's quarter!"* they opened fire at pointblank range. They would have massacred their prisoners had Colonel Campbell not begged them not to become murderers.

Only two hundred of Ferguson's men escaped; the others were killed or captured. The prisoners received rough justice; nine were tried for crimes against civilians and hung on the spot. The twenty-eight American dead were sent home for proper burial. The three hundred Tory dead were dumped into shallow pits, although they didn't stay buried for long. When Private Collins returned a few weeks later, he found thousands of bones scattered about the hilltop. Wolves had dug up the bodies and grew so bold from eating the flesh that they lost their fear of humans, making it dangerous for settlers to venture out at night.

Although no one knew it then, Ferguson's defeat was

the turning point of the war in the South. Before Kings Mountain, the patriots seemed unable to do anything right. Despite terrible hardships and setbacks, they never lost a major battle after Kings Mountain.

The tide began to turn when Nathanael Greene took over from Gates. This thirty-eight-year-old Rhode Islander was a remarkable man, having taught himself the art of war by reading everything he could find on the subject. He learned well, rising from private to major general in less than five years. George Washington called him "Brother Nat." He was his favorite field officer, as bold as Benedict Arnold, and a better man.

Although Washington couldn't spare many reinforcements, Greene's aides were first-rate. His second-in-command was the "Old Wagoner," Daniel Morgan. His cavalry commanders were "Light-Horse" Harry Lee and William Washington, the general's cousin. Thaddeus Kosciusko served as chief engineer.

Brother Nat had a plan in mind when he came south in December 1780. He didn't want to challenge Cornwallis in an all-out battle, but to keep him off balance, steadily wearing him down. Greene alone would decide when and where to give battle. He'd attack Cornwallis's supply lines, forcing him to chase him through the Carolinas, but fight only on his own terms. This wasn't a strategy that allowed the enemy room for error. Every time he made a mistake, Greene would be there, ready to pounce.

Greene split his forces between himself and Dan Morgan, a strange tactic, for generals weren't supposed to divide their strength in the face of a superior enemy. Yet this was a good plan, for he'd actually given the enemy two choices, both of them unpleasant. If Cornwallis struck at Greene, Morgan could slip past to strike British outposts in South Carolina. But if he went after Morgan, Greene could attack Charleston. Cornwallis decided that he had to split his own force. While he went after Greene, Bloody Ban Tarleton would deal with Morgan.

*"Brother Nat"—Major General Nathanael Greene—was one of Washington's favorite officers. From a painting by Charles Willson Peale.*

Tarleton caught up with the Americans near Cowpens, a clearing west of Kings Mountain, where cattle were fattened before sale in the coastal towns.

Morgan made camp after dark on January 16, 1781. A fine rain was falling as his troops huddled around campfires to cook supper and dry their clothes. They were jittery, as men are before battle, and Morgan tried to cheer them as best he could. He went from campfire to campfire, checking their weapons and joking about whatever came to mind. The Old Wagoner would crack his whip over Bloody Ban in the morning, he promised. If every man did his duty, "the old old folks will bless you, and the girls will kiss you for your gallant conduct!"

The armies, each about eleven hundred strong, met in the morning. Tarleton, as usual, opened the battle with a slashing attack. His cavalry, mostly dismounted and fighting as infantry, charged the waiting Americans. As the human wave rolled forward, Morgan ordered his men to fall back and re-form. It was no retreat, but Tarleton's troopers, thinking they'd already won, broke ranks and came on as fast as their legs could carry them. That's when the Old Wagoner cracked his whip.

The Americans had been running up the slope of a low hill when they suddenly turned. Hundreds of muskets spoke at once. Tories fell dead by the dozen. The wounded littered the ground, thrashing and screaming in pain. Sergeants were shouting for the survivors to re-form their ranks when a cry rose from the American line: "Give them the bayonet!"

Panic swept Tarleton's army as Morgan's infantry rushed down the slope, gaining momentum with each step. Hundreds threw away their weapons and begged for mercy on bent knees. The Americans, knowing what would have happened had the battle gone the other way, roared, "Tarleton's quarter!" It took every ounce of their officers' energy to prevent a massacre.

Tarleton himself was lucky to escape with his life. He was riding away with two officers when William Washington's cavalry charged from behind the hill. The moment Washington saw Tarleton, he led his officers toward him with drawn sabers. Washington slashed at one officer, but his saber broke off at the handle. The officer was about to crack Washington's skull with his own saber when a fourteen-year-old bugler shot him with a pistol. A sergeant drove off the other officer

*Daniel Morgan, the "Old Wagoner," in frontiersman's clothes. Morgan had scores to settle with the British, having been whipped five hundred times for striking an officer during the French and Indian War.*

while Tarleton went for Washington, who turned away the blow with his broken saber. Tarleton escaped, but his legion was destroyed as a fighting force, losing all but a hundred of its men in less than an hour. Morgan had sixty killed.

Despite this defeat, Lord Cornwallis was determined to destroy the rebels. On March 15, 1781, he met Greene's and Morgan's combined forces at Guilford Court House, North Carolina. The battle raged for hours, reaching its climax in a meadow where the armies went at each other with bayonets and rifle butts. The fighting was so fierce that His Lordship ordered his gunners to fire grape shot through the ranks of his own Redcoats to halt the American charge. He called this slaughter "victory," because Greene finally retreated. But what a price he'd paid! Cornwallis lost 532 killed and wounded, nearly a third of his force and more than twice the American losses. Apart from Bunker Hill, Guilford Court House was the bloodiest battle of the Revolution.

During the months that followed, Greene fought two other battles in South Carolina—Hobkirk's Hill and Eutaw Springs—and lost them both. But losing didn't matter. What mattered was being able to keep on fighting and to hurt the enemy at little cost to himself. As Greene wrote to a friend, "We fight, get beat, rise, and fight again." Strange as it seems, the Americans won by losing.

Yet Greene's army didn't fight alone. Every farmhouse looted, every patriot murdered after surrendering, turned ordinary folks against the enemy. Southerners resisted in countless ways. You didn't have to fire a gun to hurt the enemy. You might play stupid when a British officer asked for directions, or give wrong directions, sending a patrol miles and hours out of its way. You might also help bridges collapse and trees fall "accidentally" across roads used by enemy supply columns.

Your neighbors, however, might be very violent indeed. There were hundreds of square miles in the Carolinas where the local people could never be trusted. One British report reads like an American report from Vietnam two centuries later. "The soldiers [were] received with smiles one moment, and the following instant butchered . . . by a set of people who, by their clothing and appointments, cannot be distinguished from the quiet inhabitants of the country. . . ." The night belonged to the patriots who operated in twos and threes to knife sentries and snipe at outposts. Soldiers who wandered from camp were never again seen alive.

Military messengers went with large cavalry escorts, otherwise they were fair game, even for women. One night Grace and Rachel Martin, wives of American soldiers, put on their husbands' clothes to ambush a messenger escorted by two officers. The British were tearing along a deserted road when the women rode out of the shadows, blocking the way. Surprised, with pistols aimed at their heads, the British meekly surrendered their papers, which were sent to Brother Nat.

People also joined the guerrillas. *Guerrilla* is Spanish for "little war"; that is, war fought by roving bands operating behind enemy lines. Guerrilla bands were (and are) small, usually fewer than a hundred fighters. Being small, they could hide easily, move quickly, and hit the enemy when least expected. They might ambush a wagon train here, wipe out a patrol there, and make nuisances of themselves everywhere. If they met strong resistance, they broke contact, fleeing to the mountains and swamps until ready to strike elsewhere. Traveling lightly, they lived off game or gifts from friendly people. It was essential to be on good terms with the locals, who often provided valuable information about the enemy.

The most feared guerrilla leaders were South Carolinians. Andrew Pickens formed a guerrilla band after Tories burned his plantation. A somber man—it was said that nobody ever saw him smile—Pickens led hundreds of hit-and-run raids. Thomas Sumter's men called him the Carolina Gamecock, because he was small as a fighting rooster and just as aggressive. Fort Sumter in Charleston Harbor, where the Civil War began in 1861, is named in his honor.

The father of the United States Army's Special Forces

*Francis Marion led a guerrilla campaign to prevent Lord Cornwallis from gaining control of South Carolina in the last years of the Revolution. His skillful use of hit-and-run tactics, hiding in swamps to avoid British patrols, earned him the nickname "Swamp Fox."*

was Francis Marion. Born in 1732, he was small enough at birth to fit into a quart drinking mug. A quiet, frail child, he grew into a quiet, strong man whose favorite drink was vinegar mixed with water. Marion knew the swamps of Clarendon County, South Carolina, like the back of his hand. And he knew about Indians, their ways of fighting and surviving in the wilderness. Putting the two together, and adding ideas of his own, he built the best guerrilla band in the South.

The British were bewildered by Marion's tactics. Whenever he planned a raid, he kept the target to himself until the last moment. Marching at night from one forest or swamp to another, he made camp before dawn and rested his men until getting under way again at sunset; he never used the same campsite twice. If a bridge had to be crossed near an enemy outpost, it was covered with blankets to muffle the clatter of horses' hooves. Scouts, who always went ahead to prevent ambushes, hid in the thick tops of trees, signaling with a shrill whistle that carried for miles.

Tarleton chased Marion's band into the swamps several times. But after splashing about in mud, and giving the mosquitoes a feast, he gave up the hunt each time after only a few days. "As for this damned old fox," grumbled Bloody Ban, "the Devil himself could not catch him!" The Americans were amused that their hero was compared to a fox. And that's how we remember Francis Marion: The Swamp Fox.

IN JUNE 1781, Lord Cornwallis retreated to Wilmington on the South Carolina coast to await reinforcements and plan future operations. Uncle Nat and the guerrilla chiefs had fought him to a standstill. After more than a year of hard campaigning, only Charleston and a few other ports were secure, thanks to the Royal Navy's guns and supplies. He knew that, without this access to the sea, the Americans would wear him down, forcing him to surrender sooner or later. Yet there was still a chance to win, and win quickly. If he could conquer the Old Dominion—Virginia—everything else would fall into place, he believed. Georgia and the Carolinas couldn't survive without Virginia's men and supplies, nor could Washington's army based outside New York City.

British forces were already in Virginia. In December 1780, Benedict Arnold had led sixteen hundred Redcoats, Hessians, and Tories on a rampage through the eastern part of the state. Moving along the James River, he destroyed precious supplies, wrecked Virginia's largest cannon foundry, and burned much of the city of Richmond. Governor Jefferson offered a reward for his capture dead or alive, and soon Virginia riflemen were sharpening their aim on targets representing his head.

George Washington only wanted the traitor dead. Furious that Arnold should be ravaging his home state, he sent Lafayette after him with eight hundred men. There needn't be any trial. Lafayette's orders were clear: "If he should fall into your hands, you will execute him in the most summary way." Reinforcements under Anthony Wayne and Baron von Steuben followed several weeks later.

These reinforcements were Northerners who now had their first glimpse of plantation slavery. The Northern troops were greeted near Richmond by white women wrapped in linen against the burning sun. Lieutenant William Feltman was shocked at their servants, boy slaves in their teens: "They will have a number of blacks about them, all naked, nothing to hide their nakedness." Equally shocking was a black man's head stuck on a tree on one side of the road and his right hand tied to a tree on the other side. He'd been hanged and cut to pieces for killing his master. Incidents like these encouraged many of the Northerners to demand abolition of slavery in their home states.

In the meantime, Cornwallis planned to join forces with Arnold in Virginia. Although Arnold was soon recalled to New York, Cornwallis went ahead with the invasion. Early in May 1781, after leaving a covering force in the Carolinas, he marched into Virginia. During the next two months he spread terror, looting, burning, and killing. Once he nearly captured the entire state legislature, including Governor Jefferson, in Richmond.

Lafayette was powerless to stop him, but he kept on

his trail, hoping to slow him down and get him to make a mistake. He was helped by one of Cornwallis's own servants, a "runaway" slave named James. James really was a slave who'd volunteered for a dangerous mission. For months he sent Lafayette details of Cornwallis's plans. After the war, he took the name James Lafayette; the Virginia legislature bought him from his master and set him free with a $40-a-year veteran's pension.

James's information helped Lafayette keep after the British army all summer, snapping at its flanks but avoiding a pitched battle. As the British moved through the countryside, they began the eighteenth-century version of germ warfare. A smallpox epidemic had broken out among the slaves. The British left behind thousands of infected slaves, poor people suffering terribly, in the hope of spreading the disease among the patriots. Finally, when Cornwallis had his fill of destruction, he returned to the coast to set up a base to keep open his sea links to New York. On August 1, 1781, he arrived at a tiny tobacco port on the York River off Chesapeake Bay. Its name: Yorktown.

Washington was planning to take the offensive even before Cornwallis arrived at Yorktown. A French army under Count de Rochambeau had landed at Newport, Rhode Island. A French fleet under Count de Grasse was sailing from the West Indies. Washington wanted a combined Allied attack on New York City, the center of enemy power in North America. Yet such an attack was a big gamble. British defenses were strong, manned by seventeen thousand veterans. There'd surely be a bloody battle, and the assault might fail miserably. But the Allied armies had never been larger, and the war had dragged on for too long, so Washington felt he had to take the risk.

Cornwallis's arrival at Yorktown changed everything. Here was the chance Washington had prayed for! If Lafayette could pin Cornwallis down until the Allied armies arrived, and if de Grasse could close the harbor, the war would be won with a single blow. Cornwallis's seven-thousand-man army was nearly one-third the British force in America. Losing it would cripple the enemy militarily, forcing him to make peace.

The French left Newport late in June to join the Americans near Dobbs Ferry on the Hudson. Each army came with an imaginary picture of the other that was both true and false. Their meeting surprised everyone.

The Continentals had pictured their allies as overdressed dandies who ate frogs and spent hours combing their hair. They *were* colorful as peacocks. Their uniforms were of white linen with regimental colors—pink, blue, yellow, rose, scarlet, green—on the collars and lapels. Americans gasped as cavalrymen in tall fur hats rode by on black horses with tiger-skin saddlecloths, each man armed with pistols, a curved saber, and an eight-foot lance. Their encampments hummed with music, as bands played and soldiers danced in pairs. Americans, overcoming their shyness, joined in. "Officers, Soldiers and the Americans mix and dance together," a Frenchman wrote in his diary. "It is a feast of Equality, the first fruits of the Alliance." Yet there was another side to these dandies. They marched smartly, handled their weapons easily, and many had horrible scars on their faces. They were fighters.

The French were also surprised. They'd expected to find the neatly dressed, disciplined soldiers mentioned in European newspaper accounts of the war. But, at first glance, they thought them no soldiers at all. The uniformed Continentals seen in old drawings and paintings existed only in the artists' minds. Nearly all the men the French met wore homespun or sweat-stained hunting shirts. Most went barefoot and their hair hadn't had a barber's attention for months. They carried light packs and slept on the bare ground or in four-man tents on branches covered with dirty blankets. Many were boys of twelve or thirteen and old men. Yet their muskets gleamed and they knew how to use them. "I cannot insist too strongly how I was surprised by the American army," wrote a French officer after a skirmish. "It is truly incredible that troops almost naked, poorly paid, and composed of old men, children, and Negroes should behave so well on the march and under fire."

Today, the nine thousand men of the Allied armies could be airlifted to Virginia in an hour, along with their baggage and equipment. But in that summer of 1781, the journey took at least a month of steady marching. Those weeks on the road worried the commander in chief. For if the British learned his objective in time, their fleet could either reinforce or rescue Cornwallis. Thus, Sir Henry Clinton had to be kept in New York, and the way to do that was to convince him that the Allies would attack him and not Cornwallis.

Washington dug deeply into his bag of tricks. He planted odd bits of information, innocent in themselves, but together forming a false picture of his intentions. Troops burned barricades and filled holes in roads leading to New York. Hundreds of small boats were gathered along the Hudson. Bread ovens were built at Chatham, New Jersey, a few miles above Staten Island. Agents spread rumors in New York as well as in the Allied camps, where they were sure to be overheard by British spies. But Washington alone knew the truth, and he told nobody, not even his own staff; they'd learn their destination when he was ready to tell them and not a second before.

Washington enjoyed his role in the farce. While on an inspection tour in New Jersey, he questioned a Tory farmer about Staten Island. He suddenly stopped and, apparently annoyed that he'd said too much, told him to forget their conversation, knowing he'd do just the opposite. He also wrote long letters intended for enemy eyes. One day a messenger was captured with the general's mail pouch. Some of the letters were on homely subjects, like a request to his dentist for tools to fix false teeth. There was a letter to his nephew, Lunt Washington, warning that British raiders might visit Mount Vernon. And, best of all, there was his report of a meeting with Rochambeau where they decided to go to Virginia if an attack on New York proved impossible. All this "information" convinced Sir Henry Clinton that he'd soon be in action.

*Washington's ragged Continentals parade through Philadelphia on their way south to trap Lord Cornwallis at Yorktown.*

On August 20, Washington left a small force to cover New York and crossed the Hudson with the main Allied armies. Once across, the columns turned south, moving like lazy snakes with their heads twenty miles beyond their tails. The British braced for the attack that didn't come. As the Allies passed from New Jersey into Pennsylvania, they realized that it never would come—in New York.

Soon the armies were parading through the narrow streets of Philadelphia, where Washington's welcome amazed the French. Men and boys cheered, tossing their hats into the air. Mothers held up small children for a glimpse of their hero. Crowds pressed around him, overjoyed merely to touch his boots or his horse. Already, in the people's eyes, he was the father of their country. Washington, grave as ever, nodded and, turning to a French officer, said: "We may be beaten by the English; that is the chance of war. But here is an army that they will never conquer."

On the day before the Allies paraded through Philadelphia, August 29, a British ship left Yorktown with letters for New York. As it made for the open ocean, lookouts saw a line of vessels entering Chesapeake Bay. A flag fluttered from the mast of the lead vessel: a snow-white banner with the golden lilies of France. Count de Grasse had arrived with his fleet, twenty-eight ships of the line and seven frigates led by the 110-gun *Ville de Paris,* the largest warship in the world. In addition to tons of supplies, the fleet brought four thousand troops for Lafayette. They landed near Jamestown, where the American story had begun 175 years before.

The fate of Cornwallis's army would now lie in the hands of the Royal Navy. When Clinton saw that he'd been tricked, he sent Admiral Thomas Graves south with nineteen ships of the line. Some of these leaked so badly that they were no match for the French. Besides, de Grasse didn't have to sink the enemy in order to win; driving him away was enough to doom the army in Yorktown. And that's what he did in the Battle of the Virginia Capes. For eight days, September 5–13, lines of great warships tried, unsuccessfully, to cross the *T.* When they dueled, it was at long range and French firepower had the advantage. Although no British ships were sunk, they were severely battered and had to return to New York. Silently, the jaws of the trap closed around Cornwallis.

Once the Allied armies cleared Philadelphia, the pace of the march increased. Despite the heat and choking dust, they moved fifteen to twenty miles a day. They made a beeline for Head of Elk, Maryland, at the northeastern corner of Chesapeake Bay, where ships waited to carry their heavy equipment the rest of the way. Washington grew restless as the days went by. Leaving orders for the army to follow overland, he set out with an aide and his black servant, Billy Lee, an old fox hunter like himself.

They rode like the wind, pausing only to water the horses and gulp a mouthful of food. They made the sixty miles to Baltimore in a day and were off before dawn the next morning. Only sixty-five miles to go. Gradually, the scenery changed, became more familiar. They galloped along familiar lanes, across familiar bridges, past familiar houses. Men, recognizing the general, doffed their hats and bowed; women curtsied. Then the driveway lined with trees he'd planted with his own hands; the big house on the hill: Mount Vernon. For the first time in six and a half years, George Washington was home.

Within a week, the Allied armies were massed at Williamsburg, Virginia's capital. Washington had a warm reception when he rejoined them.

When preparations were completed, the armies marched the twelve miles to Yorktown. Washington knew the town well. He'd visited it many times to ship his tobacco and, as a young man, to bet on cockfights. After the troops made camp, they dug trenches and Henry Knox set up his cannon behind huge mounds of earth. The French had been generous, providing batteries of twenty-four-pound naval guns and heavy mortars.

Everything was ready by October 9. At five o'clock in the afternoon, Washington fired the first cannon shot in the siege of Yorktown. Instantly, every Allied gun boomed and every man cheered. This was the moment they'd waited for, fought for, suffered for, since 1775. Years later, Joseph Plumb Martin, who'd become a sergeant, recalled his feelings: "I felt a secret pride swell in my heart when I saw 'the Star Spangled Banner' waving majestically in the faces of our implacable adversaries; it appeared like an omen of success."

That feeling was shared by thousands of soldiers, including Washington. He rode everywhere, exposing himself to enemy gunners and to the stray shot that has taken the life of many a brave man. Once, while riding with his staff, British cannonballs plowed the earth near the horsemen. Everyone galloped to safety, except the commander in chief, who calmly sat on his horse, scanning the enemy lines through a spyglass.

*The surrender at Yorktown as painted by John Trumbull.*

He and his aides later came under fire during an artillery duel.

"Sir," said Colonel David Cobb, "you're much too exposed here. Hadn't you better step back a little?"

"Colonel Cobb," snapped Washington, "if you are afraid, you have the liberty to step back." Nobody dared run for cover after that. The common soldiers repeated these stories in their trenches. They were forever dodging bullets, and it was good to know that the general took his chances like everyone else.

The fury of the bombardment increased as more gun batteries were brought into action. Finally, one hundred guns were blasting Yorktown without letup. The effect was awesome. One by one the British guns fell silent, leaving the town defenseless. Buildings collapsed, burying soldiers in their ruins. Soldiers were blown to bits and chunks of flesh lay unburied in the streets. Fires raged out of control. A lucky shot caused a chain-reaction explosion among the ships trapped in the harbor. The French shot a red-hot cannonball, which, skidding along the water like a flat stone, slammed into the forty-four-gun HMS *Charon*. As *Charon* burned, she slipped her anchor and drifted into two other vessels, setting them ablaze. Onlookers said Yorktown was as close to hell as they ever hoped to be. Lord Cornwallis agreed.

The bombardment was in full swing when a redcoated drummer boy climbed upon a wall. At first, his long rolls were drowned out by the thundering cannon. But gradually Allied gunners noticed him and ceased fire. A lone drummer was the traditional signal for a parley. The British commander had decided that further bloodshed would be useless. He wanted to surrender. It was October 7, 1781, four years to the day after Burgoyne's surrender at Saratoga.

Two days later, the Allied armies formed two lines outside Yorktown. At the agreed time of 3 P.M., British and Hessian troops marched out of the town. Their flags were furled and cased as a symbol of surrender. Their muskets were unloaded and without bayonets, also signs of defeat. As they drew near, their bands began a somber, funeral-like, tune called "The World Turned Upside Down." It was quite popular, and everyone knew the words:

> *If ponies rode men and if grass ate cows,*
> *And cats should be chased into holes by the mouse. . . .*
> *If summer were spring and the other way round,*
> *Then all the world would be upside down.*

Their world *had* turned topsy-turvy. War is always hard. It is hard on the victors; but they at least have gained something, if only the satisfaction of winning. It is hardest on the losers, who have nothing to show for their efforts and sufferings. That didn't matter to the Hessians, for the Revolution was never their war. However it ended, they'd be sent home with their loot, and that was all they wanted. It was different with the Redcoats. It wasn't enough for them to go home with their skins intact; proud, brave men, they felt sure they were better than any Continental or "Froggie," as they called Frenchmen. As they marched between the assem-

*Washington's farewell to his officers at New York's Fraunces Tavern. An engraving based on a painting by Chappell.*

bled Allies, many went with downcast eyes. Some put their hands over their faces, sobbing, the tears rolling between their fingers. Officers cried openly when the time came to order their men to lay down their arms. The Allied troops understood their sadness, and they neither cheered nor said anything to make them feel worse.

Everyone understood the meaning of Yorktown. When news of the surrender reached London, Lord North staggered as if shot. "Oh, God!" he gasped, flinging his arms apart. "It is all over!" Although the war officially continued, the armies did no more fighting after Yorktown; the only bloodshed was in the west, where Tories and Indians continued to raid settlements. Lord North resigned as prime minister and a new government was formed to make peace. After nearly two years of negotiations, the Peace of Paris was signed, September 3, 1783.

IT WASN'T NECESSARY for George Washington to fight his way into New York. On December 4, 1783, he rode through the city, evacuated just days before by the British. His officers waited for him at Fraunces Tavern near the tip of Manhattan Island. It was a meeting he'd dreaded, a meeting for saying good-bye.

The long table was set with dishes of cold meats. Struggling to control himself, Washington tried to eat, but the food wouldn't go down. Trembling, he looked at the officers, men who'd been with him through so much. The room fell silent. Every eye was fixed on the general. He took a glass of wine and wished them good health and long life. Then, in a choked voice, he said: "I cannot come to each of you, but shall feel obliged if each of you will come and take me by the hand."

Henry Knox stepped forward. Washington put his arms around his friend and, crying openly, kissed him. Then each man in turn came up to his chief for a handshake and a hug. By now everyone was in tears. When they finished, the general left for the boat ride across the Hudson and the journey back to Mount Vernon.

The American Revolution was over. But as George Washington knew, that was the easy part. Now came the task of building a new nation, of molding thirteen separate former colonies into a truly United States of America.

# Some More Books

*There are thousands of books on the American Revolution. Here, I think, are some of the best. They are interestingly written and contain valuable information.*

Auger, Helen. *The Secret War of Independence.* Boston: Little, Brown & Co., 1955.

Bakeless, John. *Background to Glory: The Life of George Rogers Clark.* Philadelphia: J. B. Lippincott Co., 1957.

———— *Daniel Boone.* Harrisburg, Pa.: Stackpole Co., 1965.

———— *Turncoats, Traitors and Heroes.* Philadelphia: J. B. Lippincott Co., 1959.

Bill, Alfred H. *Valley Forge: The Making of an Army.* New York: Harper, 1952.

Bird, Harrison. *Attack on Quebec: The American Invasion of Canada, 1775.* New York: Oxford University Press, 1968.

Boardman, F. W., Jr. *Against the Iroquois: The Sullivan Campaign of 1779 in New York State.* New York: McKay, 1978.

Bolton, Charles Knowles. *The Private Soldier Under Washington.* Williamstown, Mass.: Corner House, 1976.

Bowen, Catherine Drinker. *John Adams and the American Revolution.* Boston: Little, Brown & Co., 1950.

Brown, Wallace. *The Good Americans: The Loyalists in the American Revolution.* New York: Morrow, 1969.

Callahan, North. *Daniel Morgan: Ranger of the Revolution.* New York: Holt, Rinehart & Winston, 1961.

Chidsey, Donald Barr. *The Great Separation: The Story of the Boston Tea Party and the American Revolution.* New York: Crown, 1965.

——— *The Loyalists: The Story of Those Americans Who Fought Against Independence.* New York: Crown, 1973.

——— *The Tide Turns: 1776.* New York: Crown, 1966.

——— *The War in the North.* New York: Crown, 1967.

——— *The War in the South: The Carolinas and Georgia in the American Revolution.* New York: Crown, 1969.

Clark, Ronald W. *Benjamin Franklin.* New York: Random House, 1983.

Clark, William. *Ben Franklin's Privateers: A Naval Epic of the American Revolution.* New York: Greenwood Press, 1969.

Clinton, Sir Henry. *The American Rebellion.* Ed. W. B. Willcox. New Haven: Yale University Press, 1954.

Coffin, Tristram P. *Uncertain Glory: Folklore in the American Revolution.* Detroit: Folklore Associates, 1971.

Coggins, Jack. *Ships and Seamen of the American Revolution.* Harrisburg, Pa.: Promontory, 1974.

Commager, Henry S., and Richard B. Morris, eds. *The Spirit of Seventy-Six: The Story of the American Revolution as Told by Participants.* New York: Harper & Row, 1975.

Davis, Burke. *The Campaign That Won America: The Story of Yorktown.* New York: The Dial Press, 1970.

——— *George Washington and the American Revolution.* New York: Random House, 1975.

Dorson, Richard M., ed. *America Rebels: Personal Narratives of the American Revolution.* New York: Pantheon, 1953.

Downey, Fairfax. *Indian Wars of the U.S. Army, 1776–1865.* Garden City, N.Y.: Doubleday & Co., 1962.

Dring, Thomas. *Recollections of the Jersey Prison Ship.* New York: Corinth Books, 1961.

Eckert, Allan W. *The Wilderness War.* Boston: Little, Brown & Co., 1978.

Elliott, Lawrence. *The Long Hunter: A New Life of Daniel Boone.* New York: Reader's Digest Press, 1976.

Engle, Paul. *Women in the American Revolution.* Chicago: Follett, 1976.

Fanning, Nathaniel. *Fanning's Narrative, Being the Memoirs of Nathaniel Fanning, an Officer of the Revolutionary Navy.* New York: DeVinne Press, 1912.

Fleming, Thomas J. *Now We Are Enemies: The Story of Bunker Hill.* New York: St. Martin's, 1960.

Flexner, James T. *George Washington.* 2 Vols. Boston: Little, Brown & Co., 1967.

—— *George Washington in the American Revolution.* Boston: Little, Brown & Co., 1968.

Forbes, Esther. *Paul Revere and the World He Lived In.* Boston: Houghton Mifflin Co., 1942.

Frey, Sylvia R. *The British Soldier in America: A Social History of Military Life in the Revolutionary Period.* Austin, Texas: University of Texas Press, 1975.

Furneaux, Rupert. *The Battle of Saratoga.* New York: Stein & Day, 1971.

Graymont, Barbara. *The Iroquois in the American Revolution.* Syracuse, N.Y.: Syracuse University Press, 1972.

Gross, Robert A. *The Minutemen and Their World.* New York: Hill and Wang, 1976.

Hargreaves, Major Reginald. *The Bloodybacks: The British Servicemen in North America, 1655–1783.* London: Hart-Davis, 1968.

Jellison, Charles A. *Ethan Allen: Frontier Rebel.* Syracuse, N.Y.: 1969.

Ketchum, Richard M., ed. *The American Heritage Book of the Revolution.* New York: American Heritage, 1958.

—— *Decisive Day: The Battle for Bunker Hill.* Garden City, N.Y.: Doubleday & Co., 1974.

—— *The Winter Soldiers.* Garden City, N.Y.: Doubleday & Co., 1973.

Labaree, Benjamin W. *The Boston Tea Party.* New York: Oxford University Press, 1964.

Malone, Dumas. *The Story of the Declaration of Independence.* New York: Oxford University Press, 1954.

Martin, Joseph Plumb. *A Narrative of Some of the Adventures, Dangers, and Sufferings of a Revolutionary Soldier.* Hallowell, Maine, 1830.

Miller, Nathan. *Sea of Glory: The Continental Navy Fights for Independence, 1775–1783.* New York: McKay, 1974.

Morison, Samuel Eliot. *John Paul Jones; A Sailor's Biography.* Boston: Little, Brown & Co., 1959.

Quarles, Benjamin. *The Negro in the American Revolution.* Chapel, Hill, N.C.: University of North Carolina Press, 1961.

Riedesel, Baroness Frederike von. *Letters and Journals Relating to the War of the American Revolution, and the Capture of the German Troops at Saratoga.* Albany, N.Y.: William L. Stone, 1867.

Thayer, Theodore. *Nathanael Greene, Strategist of the American Revolution.* New York: Twayne Publishers, 1960.

Tucker, Glenn. *Mad Anthony Wayne and the New Nation.* Harrisburg, Pa.: Stackpole Books, 1973.

Van Doren, Carl. *Secret History of the American Revolution.* Garden City, N.Y.: Garden City Publishing Co., 1941.

Van Every, Dale. *A Company of Heroes: The American Frontier, 1775–1783.* New York: Morrow, 1962.

——— *Men of the Western Waters: A Second Look at the First Americans.* Boston: Houghton Mifflin, 1956.

Van Tyne, Claude H. *The Loyalists in the American Revolution.* New York: P. Smith, 1929.

Waldo, Albigence. "Diary, Valley Forge, 1777–1778," *Pennsylvania Magazine of History and Biography,* 1897, 299–323.

Wallace, Willard M. *Traitorous Hero: The Life of Benedict Arnold.* New York: Harper, 1954.

Williams, Selma R. *Demeter's Daughters: The Women Who Founded America, 1587–1787.* New York: Atheneum, 1976.

Zobel, Hiller B. *The Boston Massacre.* New York: W. W. Norton, 1970.

# Index